Date Due

JUN. 6			
JUN. 22			
JUN. 26			
My 30 74'			
JAN 2	1988		

Running Towards Life

Books by Lisa Hobbs

I SAW RED CHINA

INDIA, INDIA

LOVE AND LIBERATION

RUNNING TOWARDS LIFE

RUNNING
TOWARDS LIFE

Lisa Hobbs

McGraw-Hill Book Company

NEW YORK   ST. LOUIS   SAN FRANCISCO   DÜSSELDORF

LONDON   MEXICO   SYDNEY   TORONTO

FIRST EDITION

07-029094-6

To Kay and John Monrufet

Running Towards Life

It was mid·morning and hot. No wind broke

the blue satin surface as the *Lady Rose* turned into Uchucklesit Inlet.

"That's it . . . the place with the jetty!"

My husband, Jack, standing beside me at the ship's railing, seized my arm and pointed. A quarter way up the inlet to our right was the place that was to be our home for this summer and all future summers until we could afford to retire there.

I looked at it with mingled curiosity and anxiety. It stood in a small cove at the edge of the sea like a tiny village on some wilderness sea coast—a long jetty with a railing on one side only, four bobbing floats, three small, scattered buildings and a green weatherboard cottage faced with a front verandah and wooden steps. Jack handed me the binoculars. Now I could see that there had once been a garden to the side and back of the house. Despite the spreading brambles there was a trace of discipline still—leveled areas, patches of grass, a tree or two, a yard of crumbling rock wall. Behind the house the land rose sharply to three thousand feet and culminated in a range named Mount Hecate—Hecate, goddess of moon, earth and underworld!

The inlet appeared to be about three miles long and one mile wide. At its end, a layer of rugged mountains, their peaks covered in snow, towered like a cardboard cutout: The lower slopes dropped swiftly into the sea. On all sides the inlet was thickly timbered in cedar, balsam, hemlock and fir. Even at this distance the land gave off an aura of mists and mystery; there was no sign of life and the only sounds were the ship's throbbing and the cries of the gulls that played in its wake.

The beauty that surrounded me was spellbinding but totally alien; if it did not frighten me, at least it awed me. I had been born and raised in Australia where the heat on a summer's day turns the world into ocher, shimmering and gaping. When I married my American husband I lived in California, where the same sense of seasonal devastation, of a losing battle against a dehydrating sun, was still part of the California scene, even though our family lived in the cool clime of San Francisco. There was nothing in my experience to allow for a beating sun and sapphire water to come hand in hand with a lush greenness that in its wildest, wettest winter months neither Australia nor California could possibly produce.

The *Lady Rose* slid in beside our dock. We went down the stairs into the lounge and through the coffee shop into the hold. A crew member handed out our hand luggage through the hold's side door, and one by one we stepped down onto our dock while the ship's winch lowered the crates of luggage we had brought. Soon everything was off-loaded, the ropes between ship and dock released, and as the float heaved and rocked the *Lady Rose* pulled away. We looked up to see the captain, John Monrufet, looking down with a grin. "Good luck," he said quietly. There was a woman on deck shouting down at us. The engines were throbbing, the water churning; we strained to catch her words:

"Is this your place? I'm from Carmel—Carmel, California. But I'd give it up in a moment for this."

Her voice became more frantic, faded away:

"I'll *buy* it. If you want to sell, I'll buy it on the spot."

Jack and I looked at each other, dumfounded. We had traveled by car, plane and ferry from San Francisco to the west coast of Vancouver Island to reach a summer home I had never seen before, only to have someone offer to buy it twenty yards before I reached the front door! We burst out laughing and then there was the most incredible silence.

The *Lady Rose* had disappeared into the main channel and the five of us stood there alone—Jack and I, our sons, Crispin, thirteen, and Jonathan, ten, and Bjorke (Little Bear), our own hundred-and-forty-pound Great Dane. Before us was a cluster of buildings, beyond that the mountains and behind us the sea. Jack and the boys picked up some luggage and started off down the jetty, Bjorke bounding ahead mad with pleasure.

Wishing to be alone for a moment I stayed behind. I sensed that this could be a summer that would change our lives; that once we had lived here for two months free of the pressures that dominated our lives in San Francisco there could be no returning to the old ways. Looking at the mountains and the sea and the cottage at the end of the old boardwalk, I could understand why Jack had responded and why he had bought the property at first sight. With this knowledge was the realization that if he dropped all rational processes and followed his heart, he would want to move here permanently, not in the unknown future but now, this very summer. And, for reasons which will become clear as this story is told, I had no wish to do so.

I resolved, nonetheless, to leave myself totally open to new smells, sights, sounds, experiences, and, to some extent, let the future look after itself. The whole world around me was mulch for my soul, a feast to be savored, a blessed time in which our family would be totally free from all outside obstruction and would hopefully move into a warmer, more perceptive intimacy. As it turned out, that small resolution was the first blind step towards a new life-style for all of us. I did not know that this step had been taken, nor that it would take Jack and me one full year of ambivalence, probing, introspection and, at times, fearful tension and conflict before both of us arrived at the point where we had the courage to do what had to be done.

I followed the family down the jetty hauling a share of luggage. Under the jetty planks the sunlight pierced the pale green waters to a depth of about thirty feet. The pilings were encrusted with barnacles; red sunfish and orange starfish sprawled on the brown sandy bottom. There was some kelp, with the long stalk anchored to the bottom, the fronds floating from the bulb like streamers in the wind, and close to the shore were clusters of eelgrass. Green and yellow algae sprouted from the bottom side of everything that floated; where the tide had receded, the algae lay whitened on the rocks.

A strange, rumbling, grinding sound broke the silence. It came from a little white house along the boardwalk, a house almost buried under clumps of white Easter daisies and masses of cyclamen and purple fuchsia, a whimsical building, like a fairy house in a children's book. All the windows were of different styles and sizes, and while one side of the hut was of shingles, the other was of shiplap. The third side was made of bat and board and the fourth looked like driftwood from the beach. This was the power house, and in it, looking like an iron spindle, was a Pelton wheel generator which, fed by the waters of the stream that ran by our house, would create our own electricity. Standing over the wheel were three fascinated boys of the mental age of ten—Crispin, Jonathan and their father. Jack looked up and merely pointed at the wheel; he was too delirious for speech. I went up the steps of the old house and waited on the rickety porch for the family.

With our arrival the residents of Uchucklesit Inlet now numbered about twenty people, but from where I stood facing the sea there was no sign of any life or human habitation. Half a mile to my left there was a logging camp which had temporarily closed down to lower the possibility of forest fires. Before me, and slightly to the left, was an island about one-third of a mile long; it hid the area where the inlet opened out onto Barkley Sound and sheltered our cove from the gale winds that sweep the sound in winter. Farther down the inlet to my right were two houses, and at the end of the inlet was the Uchucklesit Indian reserve, where some four or five families live, with a total number of about ten people.

Of these two houses the closest was a two-story gray stucco home which belonged to a retired tugboat captain, Bob Reynolds, and his wife, Ethel. Until a decade ago there had been a fish-rendering plant in the inlet and the Reynolds' home had been the home of the plant manager. The plant had employed over a hundred workers, all of whom lived in the company-owned village that had been erected on boardwalks over the sea and rocky shale. The postal location of the plant was Kildonan, a name given to the site many years ago by an old homesick Scot émigré.

Almost overnight the pilchards on which the rendering plant was based disappeared from the west coast of British Columbia. The plant was closed down, the inhabitants disappeared and finally, for insurance purposes, the old huts and factory were put to the torch. Only the big gray stucco home and a few pilings standing in the shallow waters remain. The post office was moved a little farther down the inlet to the home of Chrissie and Hugo Johnson, where Chrissie acted as postmistress.

All this Jack and I had gleaned from the many inquiries we made as we came down on the *Lady Rose*. As for our own property, it had an interesting history of its own. Nobody was sure when the old cottage had been built, but during the time that the fish-rendering plant was at Kildonan our property served as a marine filling station. The cottage was at least over fifty years old and somewhere on the property, "maybe on one of the hills somewhere," was a concrete pad on which two great fuel tanks had stood. After the plant closed the marine station also closed, and the house was used as a bunkhouse for loggers before being sold to a succession of private parties.

There are maps still in circulation where our property is marked as a marine filling station, and no summer passes without one or two boats pulling into our dock with a request for gas.

When the boys and Jack emerged from the power house we went into the cottage. It was a Rube Goldberg nightmare and I loved it. Here I could muddle endlessly with housekeeping and none would be the wiser. Each owner had changed the one-bedroom house to his own taste. One doorway had been filled in with shelves; a brick fireplace had been added and someone had painted the bricks pink. The back wall of the kitchen had been opened and a strange little room added. The stairway to the loft looked like a fireman's ladder, and the windows of the kitchen opened onto a porch that had no windows.

All the walls, with the exception of the living room, were of V-groove construction, a type of finish that went out of style half a century ago and is now too expensive to use. In the living room someone had covered the V-groove walls and ceiling with varnished fir plywood. As a final touch, a mysterious hand had added a series of false ceiling beams made of thin boards.

The kitchen was beyond redemption. All I can say in its favor is that the former owner had left it as neat as a pin and scrupulously clean. This was true of the whole house, which had been purchased furnished. Standing in one corner, black and ugly, was "The Black Beast"

as I soon came to call it, an antiquated wood-burning
stove on which I was to spend what seemed like one
thousand years of my life, but which was actually only
one year. When we finally drowned the Beast, I chuckled
spitefully for hours.

There was cold running water but no hot water unless
the stove was in use, as the hot-water system was attached
to it. There was never enough water for a hot bath unless I cooked a large meal; then both events occurred
simultaneously. As I announced dinner I would also ask:
"Anyone for a bath?" which seldom failed to make our
city house guests titter nervously. Their nervousness
would not be assuaged by seeing the appetite of our
sons; torn between hunger and dirt, fearful of leaving
the table lest all be gone on return, they would usually
stay at the table to eat and after a few days would be
driven into the sea for purposes of hygiene.

The bathroom was fairly modern, painted turquoise
with V-groove walls, a sink with running water, an old-
fashioned cast iron bathtub with claw feet (the boys
said it had walked to Kildonan over the mountains),
and a toilet that actually worked. These days it howls
like a foghorn when flushed, but at the time I speak of,
it was merely an efficiently functioning porcelain bowl.

There was a small loft upstairs, large enough for two
beds, and reached, as previously mentioned, by scaling
a swinging wooden ladder and shoving the ceiling out
of the way above one's head. The trap door was attached
to some chains and weights and getting in and out of
the loft could be compared only with climbing in and
out of a yawing submarine. We kept the trap door closed

at night lest anyone getting out of bed in the night drop
through to the kitchen.

Our bedroom was sunny and pleasing. It had a dark
hardwood floor, V-groove walls in turquoise, a homemade wardrobe covered in yellow cloth. The window
faced the boardwalk so that when one stood there the
eye scanned the walk to the power house, past the boat
shed, onto the jetty and out to the sea. Just outside the
window to the left was an old bower, lurching under
masses of honeysuckle, the tendrils curled around the
base of the window. The air in the bedroom was sweet
with the smell of the blossoms. The stream that ran
through gray boulders from the mountains to the sea
passed close to the back of the bedroom and I thought,
and was not wrong, of the many nights when I would
fall asleep listening to its varying melody.

While I was still poking around and hanging up
clothes on a score of wire hangers, Jack appeared looking slightly distraught. He said he had been under the
house where the wood and some tools were kept and
wanted me to come down for a look.

Apparently, building and changing the house had
not been the sole occupation of the many former owners.
As they came and went they brought with them material
for building houses, boats, power plants, fish-treating
equipment and furniture. None of it had been thrown
away. In the most incredible disarray were spare parts
for anything; nuts, bolts, washers, screws, nails, wire,
cable, rope, pipe, sheet metal, water tanks, pully belts,
axes, picks, fishnets, net floats, boom poles, washtubs,
buckets, stovepipe, canning jars, paper bags, paper

boxes, cut lumber, power saws, power-saw chains, fire extinguishers, horseshoes, books, old coins, rubber bands, and many, many balls of string. I cite only the identifiable articles.

After we had recovered sufficiently, we returned to hauling luggage and getting our household into some sort of order. Despite the spotless condition of the house, there was a good deal of hard work to be done by all of us. At every step of the way the unexpected would happen. For instance, when I turned on the tap in the kitchen sink to taste the pure mountain water that I had heard praised so highly, nothing happened for a moment. And then from the woodshed under the floor came a quite dreadful sound as if a mob of people had arisen and were clumping about in hobnailed boots. At last from the faucet came a hiss of air, a strangulating gurgle and a stream of dark-brown fluid.

Jack came into the kitchen with Crispin and Jonathan following in the position they were to assume for the rest of the summer—two inches off his heels or, if he stopped abruptly, on top of him. He said that the water was passing through half a century of rusty iron pipe, galvanized pipe and copper and plastic pipe, held together by nineteen valves from the tap to halfway up the mountain.

"There must be fifty dollars' worth of scrap brass in the valves alone. If you went out to buy them you'd pay three hundred dollars. Two valves would have done the trick."

When the water finally came, ice-cold and pure, it was as sweet as nectar. Just drinking it made you feel healthy. Mentally we had already gone into the pure-water bottling business when Crispin bounded into the kitchen: "Hey, Dad, the creek's gone dry."

We hurried out; water was running from the pipe at the side of the powerhouse but the creek was silent. "What on God's earth has happened?" Jack's voice was as dry as the creek bed. We all turned to follow with our eyes the course of the stream down the mountainside. Moments before there had been a constant fall of water over gray boulders whose tops were carpeted with moss; now there was a miserable dribble. To have our own creek was a dream we had shared for years. When we found that the flow was of such volume in the creek on our new property that we could make our own hydro-electricity, we had been enchanted. Now we stood too astonished for words. Could it be . . . a thought came into Jack's mind but he dismissed it. And yet, we had experienced already one or two malicious quips about being "another American family taking over Canada's best land." (The whole one and a half acres of it!)

"Do you think . . . that's what has happened? I bet the owners of the logging camp down the inlet have done it. They knew the property had changed hands recently to Americans and they did what they've wanted to do for years . . . diverted our water onto their own land."

This notion was even more astonishing than the fact of the disappearing water. Then Crispin spoke: "Maybe it's just that all the water is going through the pipe to the water wheel, leaving none for the creek bed."

He gave a silly grin as he said it. It was obvious that this was all that had happened. The pipe down the mountains that carried water to the power house was somehow draining the creek bed high above the house.

We sat down on the dry boulders. It was lovely sitting there in our own creek bed looking out over the sunlit inlet.

"For a moment I thought there was some sort of conspiracy. . . . All my life I've dreamed of having a creek of my own . . . that's what comes of being born and raised in Los Angeles . . . and just as I had it, it seemed somebody was waiting there to take it away," Jack said.

After a while I saw that the shadows were lengthening; if there was going to be any dinner, the Black Beast had to be attended to. Having spent a lot of my childhood in the Australian bush, I knew exactly how much loving care that great, gaping maw demanded. The men, of course, loved a wood stove in the kitchen, quite apart from the fact that there was no other means of cooking. They loved the glow, the warmth when they got up in the morning, the aroma of a big saucepan of boiling coffee, or the hissing pot of water for the tea. Nothing like a wood stove, they would say after a visit to the city, warming their backsides before going out in the cold, starry morning.

I knew enough about wood stoves to ask or give no quarter. I looked the damn thing right in the eye; it stood lumpish and unmoved. If we were going to keep our wood stove, this was going to be an Equal Opportunity household. Everyone would get an equal opportunity to get it going in the morning, stoke it during the day and clean it up at night.

From all sides I was getting static about dinner. I lit the paper and kindling that Jack had put in and hissed at the Beast: "I hope you melt."

Our first day at Kildonan ended both late and bathed

in delicate colors. It was not until ten o'clock that the sun passed behind the mountains at the head of the inlet. Once there, there was still another hour of kaleidoscopic pinks until just the frosted cones of the mountains were dipped in apricot, the waters changed from blue to gray to ink, and the mountains became a black-velvet screen standing stiff against the faint glow of the nearly midnight sky.

We ate a slow dinner by kerosene lamps, which give a warm, soft light and a touch of mystery with their shadows and flickers. When the air became a little chill we lit a wood fire in our pink-brick fireplace, reading a while to the boys before they went off to bed. They chose to sleep in the guest cabin, a small, roughly built hut twenty yards from our kitchen door.

The dog, knowing a good log fire when he saw one, stayed with us, stretched out like a tiger across the living-room floor. Bjorke is a brindled Dane with clearly marked black stripes on his reddish-brown coat. Despite massive fangs and heavy jowls he is a shameless coward. The only exception to his total commitment to a policy of safety first is his attitude towards me. I was soon to find that when I was alone on the property Bjorke adopted an entirely different stance towards the world. To the casual boatsman pulling in for water or gas he was a prancing, tense force with one object only in mind —to keep himself between me and all strangers. There is no growling, no display of bad manners or savagery; he merely prances before me, practically on my toes, pressing his body against me while he faces the stranger and I attempt to make light conversation.

With midnight upon us, we went to bed. What darkness and what silence! The glass in the window could have been a sheet of black velvet. The garden, the board-walk, the inlet had disappeared and in that darkness was all the beauty and the mystery of the universe. As for the silence, it was primordial; this is how the world must have been before fish and fowl were created.

My profound thoughts were interrupted when Jack stubbed his toe on the bathroom door and broke the silence with a fitting expletive.

"Come on, you poor old thing." I held out my arms and he slid in as if I had said the nicest thing. Despite our weariness, we lay talking for a long time. There was a quality of aloneness and loneliness in that dark-ness and silence that we had not experienced before. It was subduing. We thought of the millions of people who do not know what darkness or silence is, of the children in New York City and Los Angeles who have never seen the stars. Darkness, silence and the stars have been a critical component in the cultural genesis and evolution of man. Our mythology is rich with the mysteries of the moon, sun, stars and the planets. Out of the depths of darkness such as this came primitive religions with their harvest of rites and superstitious fears. Our genes, the twentieth century notwithstanding, are stamped with this legacy of a heaven filled with spirits and forces that control our destiny. It is more than possible that the present upsurge of interest in astrology results from the heavens being hidden under a layer of smog. As the realities of the natural world recede we return to the mysteries in the heavens. The stars are in our genes; if we cannot see them, then we must read about them in a book. A child growing up in a crowded city who has never seen the stars is as much a victim of "progress" as the trumpeter swan or the bald eagle or the salmon whose destiny is to follow the life pattern in the genes even if this results in death. The child who cannot see the stars because of factory smoke will not suffer bodily death, as does the salmon fulfilling its life cycle in a sea of diluted chemicals, but who or what can measure the damage that has been done to its soul, and to the souls of the other many millions of Los Angeleans, New Yorkers, Chicagoans whose ears are never free of sound or whose eyes can never rest from light?

Jack was still talking when I fell asleep; for eight hours I existed unconscious in a dreamless trance. I awoke to a fluttering against the windowpane, and almost cried aloud with joy when I saw it was a hummingbird. No bigger than a child's finger it hovered seemingly motionless in the air, its body shimmering green and gold as its long needle beak drew the nectar from the honeysuckle. The inlet was glass-smooth, the tide moving slowly out. I could see Bjorke sniffling along the seashore, poking under rocks with his big snout, pushing them aside with a long, stiff leg when his nose couldn't do the trick. Then I saw him push his head onto the sand quickly and crunch his jaws; he was having small crabs for breakfast.

There was something about the languorous attitude of the plants and the sea and the trees that spoke of a coming hot day. But the bedroom was cold. I slipped into cold clothes and went into an icy kitchen to get the coffee going. An hour later the bedroom door opened . . .

"There's nothing like a kitchen warmed by a wood stove and the smell of freshly made coffee."

I turned, I suppose with an abruptness that was a warning, from the stove; but Jack was grinning. The opportunity had been irresistible, he said.

When I awoke the following morning, the wood fire was already on. And so was the coffee—but on a gasoline camp stove given us by friends in Kentfield, California, who obviously had had more experience with wood stoves than we would ever have.

B<small>EFORE</small> going further with our story I should explain how we, a San Francisco family, happened to find ourselves, in the summer of 1967, resident owners of this unique homestead on Vancouver Island.

Like most city dwellers, we had talked for many years about buying a piece of property away from the city, but it seemed we never had sufficient money to purchase anything in California that would provide a sense of isolation, of distance between us and freeways, noise and the increasing pressures of population.

Every fourth weekend or so we would take off and explore the coast of California, north or south of San Francisco, looking for our Shangri-la, only to find that real-estate developers had arrived there before us. The land that was available was either too expensive or came in handkerchief-sized plots with a freeway, drive-in movie and shopping mart a step in time behind.

We searched the newspapers and every day read advertisements of land for sale in places like Arizona,
Florida, Hawaii, Honduras, the Fiji Islands and even
on the Greek Islands in the Mediterranean. To some
extent these advertisements sapped us of the strength
to look for ourselves. We came to feel that if land as
far away as the Fiji Islands was being sold by pro-
moters through the daily newspapers to land-hungry
Americans, there must be little left close to home except
at a very high price.

There were times when we felt sufficiently desperate
to regard these properties as possibilities. But like the
seacoast retreats being developed north of San Francisco, they were always expressed as "lots" and we concluded that nothing was to be gained by moving from a
suburb in California to a suburb in Honduras.

At this time we thought of such a property as a summer house only, something that could be built into a
retirement home later on. There was no thought of leaving San Francisco where we both had good jobs and a
proverbial "bright future." I was a columnist with the
San Francisco Examiner and Jack, who worked as a
civil engineer for many years before becoming a schoolteacher, was head of the science department at a private
high school.

We felt that if we could get completely away from
the city every summer, we might be able to save our souls.
We especially wanted to get away from the automobile
with its noise and smell and insatiable demands, away from
its gross bulk and position of dominance, and from all
the talk about this year's model and last year's model—
people having cars as the pioneers had children. Yet it

was more than wanting to get away; we wanted to *arrive at, arrive at* a place where the air and water would be pure, where we would be free of the automobile, where the children's brains and eyes would be free of the violence of television, where we could touch, taste, smell and feel the realities of various life forces of which we were but one form. We wanted to find ourselves, discover who we were without our interiors and exteriors being hidden behind a mask. We had no illusions that we could find a place in which we would be totally divorced from the twentieth century nor did we wish to be. We simply wanted to find a place which would give us the privacy and leisure necessary *to experience* being alive.

It was in this mood that we purchased, in 1966, a hectagonal-shaped cedar-and-glass house high in the hills south of San Francisco outside a small town named Brisbane. Each city has its scapegoat district, a foil for its own real or imagined perfections, and Brisbane served as such for exotic San Francisco, which dumped its garbage on man-made flatlands on a part of the Bay that is within Brisbane's city limits.

No matter that the garbage was all coming from San Francisco, where it was judiciously scattered throughout the city, nor that the stench of the flatlands never reached the town, let alone the surrounding hills. Mention of the word "Brisbane" was, and probably still is, sufficient to make a native-born San Franciscan quiver with mingled mirth and superiority. The garbage was not solely responsible for this reaction. For the first half of this century Brisbane served the seamier side of San Francisco's needs by providing prostitution, whiskey,

abortions and gambling fifteen minutes from San Francisco police headquarters. When the Brisbane municipal
authorities first contracted to take San Francisco's garbage a decade or so ago, it was merely carrying on an
established tradition.

We bought a house in the hills around Brisbane because we found one with more beauty and privacy than
we could afford to purchase elsewhere. Myth, snobbery
and history had not only kept the masses out but the
land values down. For $38,000 we bought a house on
a quarter-acre lot that ended in a canyon thick with
madrones and bay trees, a spellbinding view of the San
Francisco-Oakland Bay, and all the privacy we could
wish for at the end of an unmade country lane.

The former owner, who held title to a lot next door,
assured us prior to purchase that he would not build
for years. Within two months of our moving in he started
construction of a house that came, in places, fifteen feet
from our bedroom window. We said nothing either to
him or to each other, just passively watched it go up
with quiet despair. Jack could exist for a time without
the reality of privacy and beauty; he had been doing that
for ten years. But he could not exist without the hope
that there would be more to his existence than an entire
lifetime spent locked within a fluorescent, noisy, smelly,
overcrowded man-trap. My hopelessness grew because it
was obvious that in our traditional marriage it was I in
the image of wife, mother and homemaker who robbed
Jack of the freedom necessary to restructure his life in
a freer, more natural environment.

When Jack was sixteen he had left his home in Los
Angeles and gone north looking for work. His search

took him through Oregon and Washington over the
border into Vancouver, Canada. There a logging agency
found him a job working at the Franklin River Camp
on Vancouver Island, an experience that opened up a
new world to him. He had crossed to the island on one
of the old "Princess" ferries with its rosewood paneling,
linen tablecloths and silver service in the dining room.
From the coastal town of Nanaimo he had gone by train
northwest to Port Alberni, then caught a coastal steamer
called the *Uchuck I* to Franklin river. Once there, he
boarded a small logging train and rode along the cliffs
of the inlet to the camp site. He had never forgotten
this trip with its revelation of a physical beauty and
personal service that he had not dreamed existed before.
Now, more than twenty years later, in San Francisco he
was to once again remember it. And so it was that, during
the Easter school break of 1967, Jack drove north for
Vancouver Island looking for hope under the guise of
land.

Two days before his return he telephoned from Port
Alberni to say he had found nothing other than roadside lots or small parcels of an acre or two. Waterfront
property from the Puget Sound area of Washington
northwards was as expensive as land at Sausalito or
Tiberon on the San Francisco Bay. It was all accessible
by automobile, not remote in any true sense, and had a
tax rate as high as any in the California suburban areas.
He had traveled all over Vancouver Island looking for
something that was accessible by water and within an
hour's flying time by float plane from Vancouver. There
was nothing. The east coast of the island was fast becoming a resort area and marina serving British Co-

lumbia, Washington, Oregon and California. On the west coast so little property had been taken freehold from the Crown (meaning the Canadian Government) that the little left was not for sale. The few freehold areas that were available were all located on highways and new laws made it impossible for anyone, American or Canadian, to purchase freehold any waterfront property if the land belonged to the Crown.

Jack's tone was not disappointed; it was disappointment itself. He said that what he was wanting seemed to have gone forever, gone before anyone understood or appreciated its meaning. I urged him to keep looking until the last moment and hung up filled with a vague anxiety. Even when the hope of finding a summer place existed, the tension between Jack and me had grown with the passing of each week. It was obvious that, if Jack could not find a place of escape, the tension within our marriage might become unbearable.

I was scarcely expecting the blithe spirit who phoned the following night. He had found "the last piece of property in North America." It was perfect, just a little over an acre but surrounded by Crown land which would never be sold, so that if it were one thousand acres, it could not be more protected, more remote. He had put down $500 and what did I think? Under my breath I thanked God and aloud told Jack he was a genius.

Two days later Jack was back in the city brimming with happiness and the story of his acquisition. The morning after his first telephone call he had driven from his motel back into Port Alberni for breakfast. He was sitting in a cafeteria eating a "logger's breakfast" (a

gross quantity of pancakes, eggs, potatoes and toast),
when he noticed a sign on the weatherboard building
across the street: Estate Agent and Shipping Office.

It was now raining heavily. He dashed across the
street and into the office. Yes, there was waterfront
property for sale but it was down the inlet. The agent
took out a few snapshots—a scattering of old buildings
on a piece of land at the edge of the sea. Jack explained
he was interested in vacant land, something he could
build on after retirement. The agent assured him there
was no such land available—only this property with a
house, small guest cabin, power house and boat shed. It
also had its own jetty and floats. The owner wanted
$10,000.

After some hesitation Jack asked if he could see the
place. No. The only way there was on a ship called the
Lady Rose and it went into this inlet and Kildonan on
Tuesdays and Thursdays. And this was Friday. On
Monday Jack had to be back in his classroom, shaven,
hair combed, pants pressed. He asked about roads: Could
he drive in? And then he laughed at his own conditioning. He wanted a place inaccessible to automobiles and,
when desperate to see it, wanted to drive in.

Leisurely, the agent's brain turned. Well, if he *really*
wanted to see it, he could fly in. There was a small airline company nearby the foot of the main street, Argyle,
and it had regular flights across the island as well as
planes available for charter. Jack raced through the
rain down to the dock. A small float plane sat there
bobbing on the water, all gassed up and ready to deliver a logger to some remote boondock. Five minutes
after leaving the agent Jack was airborne in murky

clouds and driving rain, the pilot chewing gum and singing. Ten minutes out he landed at the foot of a mountain and deposited the logger on a group of floating logs. There was nothing nor anybody in sight, only the mountains, the trees, the rain and the logger. When the plane was airborne the pilot shouted: "Where to now?" and Jack roared back the instructions given him by the agent: "The first place in Uchucklesit Inlet past the logging camp at Green Cove."

There was no difficulty in finding it; the little jetty stood out bravely in the howling wind and rain. The pilot could wait no longer than thirty minutes, and during that time Jack raced around, his glasses streaming, his clothes soaked and his ears filled with the wild roar of the stream that tumbled down the hills and through the holding. He said he looked as carefully as possible, but I rather fancy that once he had seen the cottage and the power shed and jetty, and heard that mountain stream roar, all rational processes ceased. Back in Port Alberni, Jack put a deposit on the property, telephoned me and started for home.

We lay awake a long time on Jack's first night back, both knowing that something more significant than buying a summer house had occurred. Jack had left San Francisco looking like a tense and aging man; now there was a glow to his whole body and a lightness in his manner that had been gone for years. Jack had stumbled upon a life-style in the wilderness that he recognized instantly as his own; the place that the forces within him had unconsciously searched for since childhood. My relief that he had found the perfect summer home was intense, yet its very finding was somehow threatening.

We seemed to have resolved one crisis only to set things up for another. Now that we had a home in the wilderness of British Columbia, what would we do with it?

We did not bring any of this out into the open; it was too threatening for discussion. Instead, we fell asleep paying tribute to the phony rationality that dominated our lives. We spoke of going up to Kildonan each summer; of how the boys would enjoy it and what humus it would be for their memories and imagination, and of how we would gradually improve the property until our retirement there in our sixties. We lied to each other under the guise of understanding and finally fell asleep.

A little more than two months later when school closed for the summer vacation Jack drove north, taking Crispin and Bjorke and all the supplies and equipment we would need. Two days later Jonathan and I flew from San Francisco to beautiful Vancouver and crossed by ferry to Nanaimo on Vancouver Island where Jack met us. We then drove north to Port Alberni. This was a humiliating ride to say the least, as the long haul from San Francisco had been more than our vast monster of an automobile, "Moby Dick," could cope with. Attempting to flee the horrors of pollution, we found ourselves producing a cloud of dirty blue smoke which traced our progress along the highway as clearly as if we had littered the road with empty pop cans.

We were not entirely to blame as Moby Dick had not been purchased. He had come to us on the death of a Los Angeles relative. As Moby was nine years of age he was regarded in those curious parts as something of an heirloom. He was a hybrid, the end result of Detroit's attempt to cross a truck with a passenger automobile.

The front section of the vehicle was a sedan, the second section a small truck with flashing chrome, flying wings and nowhere to tie a rope. At the time of this summer trip to Kildonan, Moby had been with us for two years, still owned by our deceased relative, for he could not pass the California smog test and under the new smog laws title could not be transferred. When he came to us he was pretty much all whimsicality and soul; now, as he coughed and rattled on, his demise seemed not only desirable but highly likely.

Finally we made it over the mountains and started down into Alberni Valley. We were eager to see Port Alberni. When Jack had been through it at the time of the purchase the rain had been so heavy and the visit so hurried that no new impressions were gained. All he could remember was the Port Alberni of twenty-three years earlier—a logging town in a valley ringed by snow-capped mountains, the waters of the inlet pure and stocked with fish, the air clear and full of good smells. What a gap between memory and reality! The town we saw as we swung down the highway was dominated by a vast mill whose towering smokestacks incessantly spewed out waste. And then the smell from the pulp mill hit us, "the sweet smell of money," as the motel manager later described it. It was indescribable; we rolled up the windows, held our noses to no avail. There was no protection from the putrescent effluvium. Bjorke looked up from the floor of the car with watering eyes and a pained expression; heaven knows what he thought.

This indescribable smell turned out to be the most outstanding feature of Port Alberni. The town itself was like every other town with parking meters, taxi stands, supermarkets, used-car lots, traffic lights, service stations with revolving plastic signs, and cardboard motels. The old part of town was still there looking like its small-town American counterpart—buildings falling down or in the process of being pulled down, others standing dusty, empty and forlorn.

We walked down to the bottom of Argyle Street, past the disused railway station and the abandoned liquor store, once the pride of the town. Although it was a hot day there were no children swimming or salmon dancing from the water; it was so dark and sludgy-looking one of the boys remarked it looked like grape Kool-Aid. An old-timer sitting in the sun at the end of the wharf told us that nothing of the rich seashore life which had once flourished at the head of the Alberni Canal now remained. Each year a few salmon made it through the pollution to spawn in the small Somas River which flowed into the head; but by and large the harbor itself was little more than a sterile body of chemical preservative.

Disappointed, we started out for a local motel, as the *Lady Rose* did not sail until eight the following morning. En route we noticed a number of people stopping to stare at us. We soon found out why. Most of our gear had been unloaded at the warehouse on the dock and Bjorke put into the car's truck end. Now he stood with his front paws on the roof of the car looking as large as a horse as he moved in his chariot through his new territory. It was for this reason we quickly became known in Port Alberni as "the rich Americans with the big dog." It was true that the dog was big, but what imagination was needed to produce a rumor that we were rich!

We drove to the outskirts of town, looking for a motel as far-removed from the stench as possible. The manager of the one we chose, a thin woman with a hacking cough and bright red lipstick, voluntarily brought up the subject of the stench, first apologizing for it, then explaining quite defensively how much money the mill brought to the valley. The foul air; the fine ash, which took paint off automobiles; the polluted harbor—these were the unfortunate by-products of "progress," she said, then added: "Without the mill we'd all be dead," blissfully oblivious to the fact that the very reverse might be the truth.

Were we from California? When we said yes, another question followed: "Driving out to Long Beach by way of the new Tofino Road?"

We explained that we had a small summer house in Uchucklesit Inlet. She had never heard of it. We tried again; the house was near the post office at Kildonan. Never heard of Kildonan. This was the first of a dozen such conversations. Many of Port Alberni's residents, it seemed, were newly arrived from somewhere else and few of those who had lived there for some years had ever ventured down the canal. If they went anywhere, it was south to Victoria or across the Georgia Straight to Vancouver. With few exceptions only fishermen, loggers, tourists and Indians ventured down Barkley Sound. The factory workers, mill hands or those in the stores or service fields knew no more about the town and its environs than they knew of any place picked at random in North America, for many of them were part of that vast migration of people that started to move westward after the Second World War and is still on the move.

The next morning we had breakfast, packed, got the boys out of the motel swimming pool and drove downtown. When we found a shady spot on an unmade side street, we parked and locked the car and walked down Argyle Street to the *Lady Rose* dock.

We thought the *Lady Rose* was a fine-looking ship. She is, in fact, the very last of hundreds of coastal steamers that once served the small ports along the shores of Puget Sound in Washington State, Vancouver Island, the wide and isolated Queen Charlotte Islands and the coast of British Columbia and Alaska, bringing in the outside world in the form of wood, mail, clothing, newspapers, liquor and medicine. About two hundred tons in weight and one hundred feet long, the *Lady Rose* exudes a sense of history; only the new Canadian flag flying astern—the red maple leaf on a white background—reveals the passage of time. When the *Lady Rose* finally goes to scrap, an era will have ended.

The *Lady Rose* is owned by two ship's captains, John Monrufet and Richard McMinn. We had written from California saying we wished to go into Kildonan with luggage on this particular day, and so we were hardly under way when Captain John Monrufet introduced himself. Civilities had barely been exchanged when Jack asked the question that had been like a burr in his brain since we had seen the polluted harbor the previous afternoon: Just how far down the inlet did the pollution go?

About halfway down the thirty-eight-mile passage, said Captain Monrufet.

"The mulch from the mill is about three fathoms deep in Port Alberni and by the time it reaches Nahmint, which is eleven miles down the inlet, it is only on the

surface. When the mill is shut down for any reason it is
remarkable how quickly the water clears up; in a few
days it begins to look clear. But the way it is now, it is
terrible stuff. A friend who does a lot of diving brought
some of the sediment to the surface recently and found it
so loaded with chemicals it burned even when wet."

By now we were well under way. The early morning
fog, which is characteristic of a summer's day in Port
Alberni, had lifted, leaving wreaths around the mountain peaks and wispy tracing in the valleys. The land
on both sides of the canal was heavily timbered, creating
a blue-green world of water and sky with mountains un-
folding layer after layer until hidden by distant mists.
I was reminded of the inland sea of Japan or of one of
the gentler fiords of Norway. A few fishing boats passed,
but not many, for as the fish were exploited and the
waters polluted the importance of Port Alberni as a
fishing port had faded.

There were some seventy tourists on board—the *Lady
Rose* with its crew of five takes up to one hundred passengers—and many of these tourists were Americans.
One couple was from Arizona, and I remember their
stunned expressions at the richness of the land. As the
sun rose and the water became even bluer, a sense of
relaxation swept the passengers as if the soul-polluting
cares of the city were ebbing away in the throbbing of
the engine and the swirl of the wake.

I wish I could say that this idyllic journey continued
until we reached our destiny, but this was not so. Forty
minutes out of port, sailing south on Alberni inlet, we
passed a logged area.

"Oh, look!" a woman involuntarily cried in a shock

so genuine that the ship's passengers stopped talking
and turned in silence to look at the horror of a scalped
and lacerated mountain. It was as if a vast tapestry
depicting a scene of total destruction had been unrolled
before our eyes. This was surgery done without the
spilling of a drop of blood, surgery done on the face
of the earth with bulldozer and chain saw. Only a small
part of the devastation was visible from the ship; yet
what could be seen added up to a scene of such rape and
looting that the onlookers winced, turned away and
sought reaffirmation of the good earth in the hills opposite.

From the silvered stumps it was apparent that this
area had been logged many years previously, yet there
was no evidence of any reforestation or reseeding—a not
so uncommon case, as we were to find out later, for the
Canadian Government can demand reseeding or reforestation only on those lands it owns and leases itself.
Privately owned timberlands can be raped to the owners content and left, as this was, with its stumps forever
standing like markers in an abandoned graveyard—all
so that the nation can have a 160-page Sunday newspaper and every supermarket purchase wrapped in a
separate paper bag. For the first time I caught a glimpse
of the real price yet to be paid for our standard of living and understood how we were robbing the world,
which had nurtured and renewed itself on itself for millions of years, of all these powers of self-healing and re-
newal.

I was standing at the ship's railing in this mood when
the *Lady Rose* turned into Uchucklesit Inlet. This was
the moment in time at which I started this book and

now, having explained how and why we were in the wilderness of British Columbia, I shall return to that story.

$$\sim$$

ON THE third day of our first summer at Kildonan it became obvious that unless we had a small dam or reservoir, water could be a major problem during the dry summer months. So we decided to hike up the steep mountain behind us to check the situation.

It was early afternoon when we left and a beautiful day. The alder trees, with their full summer growth, shaded the creek from the full rays of the sun while allowing enough warmth through to give life in abundance to the heavy moss and ferns that clung to the rocks along the water's edge. For some of the way we could follow the creek bed; but at other times the course was so steep and the moss-covered rocks so treacherous that we beat our way through the tangles that covered what had once been a narrow path. Here there were none of the ferns and bracken, fireweed, stinging nettles, blackberries, wild roses and morning-glory that ran riot through our old gardens; it was tropical rain forest, totally different from anything I had expected, luxuriously springy under the feet, rich with a piny perfume, the air warm under a triple canopy of boughs.

After a time we found a smooth cluster of rocks at the bed of the creek and settled down for a sandwich

and to drink the cold, pure water. When I looked up I
was delightfully surprised, for the magic garden in which
we now sat, humming with contentment, was at the bottom of another garden, a garden comprising the tops
and branches of giant cedar, fir and hemlock, some of
which had been standing there for hundreds of years.
Bjorke, I noticed, had found a long smooth rock draped
with a sheet of moss; now he stretched against its hard
coldness with an old man's sigh of deep satisfaction. It
was hard to believe that a century might have passed
since another person had sat here, or that perhaps we
were the first humans ever to have body contact with
these gray and beautiful boulders. Hard to believe, too,
that back in San Francisco life was going on as usual.

"Right about now," said Jack, looking at the sun
(for we made a point of not wearing watches at Kildonan), "I would be working my way onto the freeway
at the Fell Street entrance." The picture conjured up
by his words—the gray freeway strips, concrete abutments, noise, fumes, speed—had, in this setting, an unreal aspect a little like the tracings of a troublesome
dream.

We resumed our climb past moss-covered stumps of
trees that had been logged many years back. There
were some trees that had fallen intact years before. We
would walk their length as the going was easy this way
but often they would crumble beneath our feet, sodden
and rotten with age. Jack pointed out the notches on
some of the stumps; the loggers of former times had cut
these notches, placed a board in them, then, standing on
the board, had felled the tree with a handsaw. By felling
this way the logger cut high enough to avoid the mottled

grain at the tree's bottom, a practice that the law no longer allows, for, quite apart from the fact that the trees are logged by power saws, the heights of the stumps are strictly limited.

We followed the creek and the old rusty pipe which ran its length down to our house. After a while the iron gave way to black plastic, then disappeared between vertical slate walls about fifty feet high. Once again we left the creek bed and pushed up through the forest, finally reaching a clearing surrounded by giant cedar trees nearly two hundred feet high and twenty feet around the base. Pink-cheeked and puffing, we slid gratefully onto the ground. Through the trees we could see small patches of the blue inlet far below us.

Crispin said he could hear water falling. We fell silent and soon, from the gorge below, the noise of falling water could be heard above the gentle humming of the wind in the trees. Jack put the coil of rope he had brought around Crispin's waist, wrapped it around his own and knotted it around a tree; then Crispin was lowered over the edge.

He reappeared in a few moments, his eyes sparkling with pleasure. There was a fine waterfall at the bottom of the gorge, he said. Just as important was the news that the plastic pipe was tied to a steel cable suspended over the gorge wall where it disappeared into the waterfall. When Jack's first reaction was that "the plastic pipe has to go," I chuckled to myself, for that had been my first reaction, too. Plastic pipe in this Garden of Eden? We all agreed as if we had laid low a common enemy.

We followed the creek to a meadow where natural

springs flowed, then descended to see if we could locate
the end of the pipe. This time we went down the creek
itself, frozen to our waists in the icy water, till we eventually found the end of the pipe lying in a natural pool.
Whatever hopes we had of finding a dam and an assured
supply of water for the summer were now gone. Crispin,
given more to honesty than to tact as children are, chose
that chilly moment to say: "Hey, Dad, thought you said
there must be a dam."

"Yeah, Dad," Jonathan piped in, "thought you said
there must be a dam."

"We're going to build a dam," said Jack. "Before
this summer is out we will build our own fine dam right
up here in the hills."

Immediately both boys burst into endless monologues
as to where the dam should be built and what type it
should be, drawing from their rich fund of inexperience.
We started retracing our steps down until we reached
a spot where we could descend to the creek and work our
way back to the waterfall. Once there, we could see from
the small fall of water that most of it was being trapped
into the plastic pipe. This meant that there was a very
real danger of running out of water should the summer
be dry and long, for we were already getting the maximum flow. There was no reserve at all. We climbed up
to the head of the fall; from here the cliff cut back under
us. In this cutback was a gorge no more than four feet
wide with vertical walls of over twenty feet. Jack thought
it was a perfect site for the building of a dam.

We built the dam that very summer. It was our major
project and, despite the modesty of the basic plan, was

difficult and time-consuming but indescribably enjoyable.

We saw that if the gorge were blocked, it would act as an ample reservoir. So working as a team we hauled several massive beams up the mountainside where Jack built them into a large-frame box. It was so heavy, there was no need to drill steel pins into the rock face to hold it in place. Once it was locked into position across the front of the gorge we started the long and tiresome task of filling it with rocks and gravel; there were ample deposits of both in a little meadow where three natural springs flowed higher up the mountain.

Jack took an old wooden box, which had once served for crating fruit, and strung it between two poles. He stayed down in the gorge while one boy at a time and myself ran up and down the mountain hauling and depositing rocks and gravel in our coolie fruit box. Once we were back at the gorge, we deposited our load onto a homemade chute which fell down into the wooden frame. Jack, half-in and half-out of the icy water below, was not only periodically splattered with our muddy gravel, but hit with rocks. I would put my load into the chute and hold my ears.

As my visit to China in 1965 was still very much part of my life, as it is today, we called our creation the Mao Tse-tung Dam of Family Harmony. The Family Harmony part was a bit much, Jack and I agreed, but we managed to laugh about it. We did not laugh much this winter, however, when, following a succession of cloudbursts, a roaring avalanche of gravel filled the dam.

The next reservoir we build, Jack says, will be called the Mao-Tse-tung Dam of Family Patience.

———⌣———

W<small>E WERE</small> sitting at breakfast on our first Sunday when we were startled out of our cumulative wits by the ringing of the telephone.

Coming in as strangers from another world, we had believed implicitly all that we were told about certain aspects of life in Uchucklesit Inlet, not the least of which was the repeated statement that there was no communication with the outside world. That in fact, the Good Friday earthquake at Anchorage, Alaska, in 1964, had created such a tidal wave in the Alberni Canal that all the telephone lines on both sides had been knocked down. The damage had been so extensive that the telephone company had decided to bring in radio telephones rather than replace the lines.

We had noticed the old black hand-cranked phone stuck on the wall when we arrived, and the boys had often picked it up, and occasionally cranked it, taking it for granted that the line went nowhere. The line, to our mind, was no more connected to the outside world than the Pelton wheel. When it rang, one long insistent ring, we were literally paralyzed. Then it rang a second, a third time. I jumped up: "I'll answer it."

Someone said: "But how do you know it's for us?"

We looked at one another. If we could have seen what

a bunch of clowns we were being, we would have been paralyzed with laughter rather than indecision. Finally, Jack declared: "Somebody's got to answer it. Answer it, Crispin."

Crispin took the receiver with the faith of one holding a walking stick to his ear: "Hello. Yes, I think so, just a minute and I'll ask."

He turned to us and said that the man on the other end wanted us to come to dinner.

"Well find out who he is, Cris."

"Who are you?" asked Cris. "You're what? The man at the other end? The other end of what?" Turning, he explained: "He says he's the man at the other end."

"The other end" turned out to be the cook at the logging camp half a mile away. The logging crew was away in town and he wanted us to share dinner with him that night. Casually, we said we would go. We gave not a thought to the distance or means of transportation, so accustomed were we to easy mobility. A half a mile was nothing! It was only after we had hung up that we began to realize we were not going to step into an automobile and drive off down a made road. It wasn't to be that easy.

When we purchased the property we found that we had also purchased three boats—an inboard clinker-built, an outboard clinker-built and a plywood skiff. The skiff held one passenger, the outboard three, and so if the five of us were going out for dinner—for there could be no thought of leaving Bjorke—the inboard had to be put into operation. We walked down the jetty to the dock with growing dismay, for the inboard rested on a float, all eighteen feet and a ton of weight. It must have been hoisted there by means of a tackle. We looked around in vain.

For someone who had done such things before, the task before us would no doubt have been quite simple. But for us, with our total hoist and tackle knowledge little more than that of stone-age savages, the task was monumental. When we removed and stored the canvas covers, we found that the float was only two feet longer and four feet wider than the inboard, little room for amateurs who had no idea what they were doing.

Finally, Jack decided to cut some small logs for rollers. Then, by our using a piece of timber as leverage, the boat was raised sufficiently high to place log rollers under it one at a time. It was then a matter of getting the boat into the water while keeping it from falling to one side.

It was actually a simple task but it gave us much to think about; for this was the only time I could remember that the four of us had been forced to work together in a sweat-producing, muscle-aching, do-or-die project. With all the talk of family togetherness, it was a togetherness, in retrospect, only present in pleasurable times, for there is little or no chance of today's modern family sharing true labor. And, when it does happen, so much emphasis has been placed on success that the most common reaction to a difficult task is to display hostility if the challenge cannot be immediately met and overcome. Indeed, a great part of society exists solely to remove responsibility from new tasks or problems which might confront one—a million experts on a million subjects who will bail us out and save the day. And so, particularly in interrelationships with one's family, we are seldom if ever tested, and much that could actually strengthen and enhance family life—such as the acknowledgment of sharing failure—is lost.

We finally got the old clinker going and off we went, put-put-put, down to the logging camp, some of us a little scratched, some hoarse from shouting—and barking—and all subdued by the sudden realization that we were together in a true wilderness and totally dependent, one on the other.

Was this our host? I put on my glasses for a better look as our clinker, with Bjorke standing in the prow like an ancient masthead, putted into the Green Cove logging camp.

The cook's hair had not been combed for a period beyond estimation; on his face was a salt-and-pepper stubble. His pants were held to his waist by a length of rope, and on his feet were old black Oxfords, minus any laces, with six inches of leg showing between shoes and pants. With a flourishing bow our host introduced himself, and waving one hand, offered a delicate hint of apology for his appearance. We walked down a rough road to the bunkhouse, a two-story building facing the sea. The men's sleeping quarters were upstairs, with the kitchen, office, bathrooms and recreation room downstairs. From the side of the bunkhouse a road wound slowly up the mountain. Trucks and massive pieces of earth-moving equipment were scattered around the yard.

There was little conversation during dinner, which we ate sitting on benches at a long wooden table. It turned out to be typical Kildonan conversation—hopeful remarks about the weather and comments on the fishing conditions. As we were getting back into our boat, we were startled by our host's warning us not to wander up the mountain the following week as a blasting crew was going in to widen the mountain road.

Jack asked: "What road?" We felt haunted by the automobile. We had traveled almost as far as one could go only to find a blasting crew preparing to bring the entire population of the Pacific Northwest to our doorstep! But our fears were getting the better of us, for it was only a logging road for the hauling out of felled trees. Nine miles long, it was still fifteen miles away, over rough terrain, from the nearest road that connected the town with Port Alberni.

"Fifteen miles," our host said cheerfully, "and before they connect we'll all be dead."

As he said this he danced a little jig, turned on his heels and waltzed back to the house. No mean feat in unlaced Oxfords.

THE days melted one into the other. Time, which dominated every minute of our lives in San Francisco, faded in importance until it had no more reality than our immediate needs invested in it. Past and future were distinguished by the arrival and departure of the *Lady Rose* two days a week. We were reminded that it was late morning and time to rise by the empty feeling in our stomach; or that it was late afternoon by the light wind which would rise and sweep across the inlet, darkening the waters and ruffling it into perfect little corrugations; or time to go to bed simply because our tired muscles would hold us upright no longer.

Lacking any need to conform to concepts of time imposed by society, we found that our natural daily peaks and lows of energy, interests and desires had no relationship to the acceptable activities and time sequences of the urban world. As our inner lives relaxed and assumed a more natural condition, we began to see the extent to which our lives in the city were controlled by forces outside us. We must arrive at work, have lunch, go home, go to school, go to bed at the same time every day. We must shop during certain hours, do our housework at certain hours, worship at certain hours, use the library at certain hours, become sick only within certain hours, if possible. Only in giving birth or dying are we fully excused for not keeping our activity within regulation hours. Removed from society, we could see that the concept of time which society has fashioned for its members bears no relationship to the vast individual variations within man. I had known for a long time that the blueprint within my own genes was quite opposed to the social norm—that I am most creative and active during the long hours of the night and most prone to sleep during the dawn and early morning.

Now, after a morning's activity I was perfectly capable of falling asleep under the morning sun and waking again in half an hour, totally refreshed. Little naps like this added a day to my life; certainly, they added many hours of wakefulness to my days. Jack was undergoing

a similar discovery, although he preferred to sleep in the
early afternoon. When we talked about this we concluded that there will be no solution to many of the
problems of individual maladjustment within our society
until the social agencies that deal with these matters
destroy the conventional restrictions of time and, at
the same time, encourage individuals to seek solutions
outside accepted social activity. For often as not social
activity is that which best serves the demands of a time
slot.

As our city attitudes towards time unfolded and relaxed, we began opening up to new natural experiences
such as the *experiencing* of rain.

Living in San Francisco, we were not without ample
experience of rain, but there it was inevitably a nuisance.
It disrupted the smooth flow of the city's tightly sched-
uled activities, ball games were canceled, school days
shortened, hair-dos ruined, clothes rumpled, windscreens
muddied, carpets dirtied and driving made hazardous.
The city person has no *need* of rain. He realizes the
farmer needs it and the hydroelectric plant must have
it but, stuck behind his steering wheel in a rain-induced
traffic jam, such considerations do little to abate resentment towards this natural phenomenon.

At Kildonan we were free for the first time in our
lives to enjoy rain. A little mud in the cottage made no
difference nor did rumpled clothes. There were no ball
games to cancel and no car to wash; unless the fall was
cold or blindingly heavy we ignored it, taking pleasure
in its sting on our skin, or the delicious smells that it
conjured up out of the clumps of fuchsia and wild
daisies, berry bushes and ferns and bracken and dan-

delions. Within minutes the creek would change from a gentle stream to a frothing white avalanche. At such times I practiced a little custom I learned in Asia. I would sit on the verandah with my eyes closed and listen to the sound of the rain, for rain makes a symphony of sound, turning each object it strikes into its own musical instrument. Plip, plop, bing, bong, splat—on the leaves of the English chestnut tree, on the pond in our garden, onto the warm earth, the boardwalk, the tree stumps, dripping in the forest.

While I was sitting one day listening to this symphony of nature, feeling it sweep soundlessly across my legs in gusts, Jack pointed across the inlet.

"I got up early this morning and there was a single cloud there, lower than the rest and tangled in the trees. I was probably still half-asleep, for it seemed in the dawn as if some immense creature from the heavens had come too close to us and been trapped by our trees and branches. I wondered how it could get away and back to its full-bodied freedom without tearing itself to pieces. Then it drifted up and away without disturbing a leaf; soon it joined the others and it began to rain again. It was very still on the inlet. The rain descended on the water like a million ballet dancers, gently at first, then, bursting into a dance of madness. The only witnesses appeared to be myself and a kingfisher, so when the dance was over I stood and applauded and shouted, 'Bravo.' "

Gradually, we were becoming one with the forces of nature; all around was evidence of the shifts and changes in our interior and exterior lives. Devoid of the props which were such a large part of our family and social activities in San Francisco, we found joy in the simplest

activities, such as beachcombing for Japanese glass floats
or hunting for blackberries.

We had heard people speak of the beauty of Barkley
Sound when we had first arrived at Kildonan. Barkley
Sound emerges from the west end of the Alberni Canal,
running about ten miles long and twenty wide, and containing some sixty islands varying from the size of a
rock to two miles in length. Most of these islands are
covered with trees, and on the western side, where they
are continually exposed to severe winds, assume fanciful
and, at times, grotesque shapes. Occasionally a seed
which has fallen onto a wind-exposed rock mutates to
form an exquisite Ming tree. Small hidden coves with
white sandy beaches are commonplace, and here, where
the water is calmer, are beds of clams, oysters, abalone
and scallops. Some of the islands turn a face of sheer
rock cliff to the Pacific, and here the water heaves and
swells and, on the slightest provocation from the wind,
turns into a pounding force.

Only two small communities, Bamfield to the south
and Ucluelet to the north, offer access to this area, so it
is in a true sense a wilderness. At the time of this writing
it is about to be declared a Canadian National Park.
Today it is possible to land on any number of these isolated islands feeling that no one has ever landed there
before, an experience that will soon be a thing of the past.

These beaches and coves are rich with beachcombers'
loot, for the winds that sweep the Pacific Ocean during
the long winter months gather before them bottles, pieces
of rope and ship hatch covers, adrift from Russian,
Japanese and Chinese ships, which expend themselves

and come to rest on the northwest coast. It was over an hour's boat ride from our cottage to these islands—an old, open and not very comfortable boat—but we were always richly rewarded. The treasure we sought was the blue-green glass fishnet floats from Japan which, breaking loose from their nets, would travel with the current until they came to rest, not along the rough shore edge but among the coarse grass farther inland, deposited there by high winter tides. Some were still laced with their hand-knotted ropes. While we would sit on the sand among the grasses, eating our picnic lunch, our fancies would take free flight and we would wonder about the artisan so far away who had blown this pretty glass balloon, and the life of the fisherman who had knotted it and taken it out to sea.

In late July, when all the flowers and wild fruits were in bloom, we took to hunting blackberries. The bushes that grew on our own property were heavily laden but were quickly depleted. They stood between the cottage and the cabin and the temptation to pick and munch when going from one to the other was too much for all of us. Besides, we had no compunction about gobbling them up while we could, for it was apparent we were only one of many competitors for the sweet, purple juice; birds, raccoons, squirrels, or deer mice were all in the berry market. We set out to find another source.

We found a jungle of wild berries in a secluded area beyond the head of the inlet. To reach it we had to sail the boat through a towering granite pass about twenty-five feet high and fifteen feet wide. Once through this pass the waters opened into a secluded, crystal-clear pool,

which was surrounded by berry-laden woods. Here we
were in competition with black bears and deer, for, although we have yet to see these creatures at this particular spot, their droppings were visible.

One day we were gathering berries there when we had
a very small but precious experience. The land we were
on was part of the Indian reservation and the fruit
rightfully theirs. We had gone to Kelly Cootes, the village
chief, and he had given us his permission, for there were
not enough women in the village anymore to pick the
rich harvest and it was better that we use it than leave
it to rot. On this particular day we were picking some
distance away from the pool when we heard two women
laughing. Unwittingly hidden behind a mass of brambles
we watched two elderly Indian women paddle slowly and
gracefully through the rocky pass, stop a moment in
the center of the pool for an animated and amusing
exchange, and then paddle out again. They were speak-
ing their Indian tongue and their canoe was a hand-
carved dugout. It was a scene out of the Pacific Northwest's history. Can you imagine the impression made on
the minds of two young American boys whose sole contact with history until then, apart from what we had
tried to give them, was the senseless violence of television?
The picture lingers on in my mind as if caught in time—
the beauty of the pool and the simple grace of the
canoeists, set against the hushed wonderment and awakening that held our sons as still as deer.

For recreation at night we made full use of the large
library of stereo tapes that we had brought. We would
select a special piece or program and decide to play it

on such-and-such a night. We would anticipate this event with as much pleasure as if we had a date, a concert to attend, or as if we were flying-in our own symphony orchestra. In this mood I would cook a special dinner, and we would dress up a little and gather in our pink-fireplaced living room with a pleasure that could be no greater in a palace; for music here seemed part of the waters and forests that surrounded us—hundreds of years in the making, and eternal. Sometimes we wanted lighter entertainment and it was then that we discovered radio, not the radio of background music or the commuter rush hour but radio as entertainment.

Soon after our arrival we found that radio station KGO in San Francisco devoted one and a half hours of its prime time on Saturday night to a program called "The Mystery Hour," all apparently British Broadcasting Company plays that must have come out of the early thirties. Without doubt, KGO put them on as a spoof in the same mood in which "Superman" or the "Green Hornet" made their comebacks. "The Mystery Hour" was no trendy spoof to us; from noon Saturday our lives revolved around that coming hour. We were tortured by what would come first—9:30 P.M. or the climatic conditions necessary for good reception.

As the summer passed the nights fell earlier; by 9:30 it was dark. We would light a kerosene lamp and leave it in the kitchen so that the living room would be lit by a gentle flickering only, and sit there with Bjorke the Dane snoring, Jack with one son beside him, me with the other—all flying free in our minds without the restrictions of visual pictures, as one Scotland Yard mys-

tery after another was meticulously dealt with. Radio
to the boys was far more engrossing than television. As
for Jack and me, we rediscovered our imaginations.

———~———

Oₙₑ day early in summer we had our first American
visitors. We could hear the sound of a motor loud enough
to know that it was coming through Seekah Pass, the
small pass between us and an adjoining island. When we
went outside we could see a cabin cruiser moving rapidly
in our direction.

On board was a family of three—husband, wife and
daughter—and the conversation went like this:

"We wondered who bought the place. Come here every
year. Always stop in and say hello. Yes, sir, they were
awfully nice people who owned this place. Shame they
had to sell. Lovely people—the best. Stopped every year
and spent a few days. Winter in Mexico and Vancouver
Island in the summer. Good fishing: prawns, oysters,
clams, abalone; you just have to know where to look.
Nothing like it in the States. For years we traveled up
the east coast of the island. Stopped anywhere and tied
up. Didn't even have to ask. Always welcome. Then out
came the 'No Trespassing' signs. New kind of people
moved in. Didn't want visitors. So we now come to the
west coast. Lovely people here. We tie up anywhere. Nobody cares. We're always welcome. Tie up here and tie

up there. You know, keep on the move. We'll spend a week on the island eating off the country and then tie up at someone's float. Have you been out to the offshore islands? Lovely place. We pick up a few glass floats every year. They're harder and harder to find. People looking all the time. The tourists come up and take them home. We've got a lovely collection at home. We spend the winter in Mexico. Have a housetrailer. Pull it to Mexico every year. There's a lovely trailer court in Guadalajara. Full of Americans. Lovely people. They all go to Mexico now. Cheaper. The trailer court has a new supermarket, drugstore, barbershop, you know, just like the States. Never have to go into town. Just pull the trailer into the park and you're home. Lovely people. Gardens and a big swimming pool with a lovely restaurant that serves good American food. Not like the States. Real service. Lots of cheap labor. Do your week's laundry for a quarter. The wife and daughter and I spend the winter in Mexico and the summer in British Columbia. We have a big place in California. Spend a few months there in the spring and fall. The race thing, you know. Mind you, we're not prejudiced. It's a matter of law and order. You're not safe there anymore. You know —you're from there. We had a letter telling us this place was sold and some Americans bought it. Wait until you spend your first winter here. Then it won't look so good. Rains a lot. This morning, those few drops were nothing. Never spent a winter here myself. But I suppose you're only here for the summer. Have you been to Bamfield? Lovely place. Lovely people. That's what's so good about the people, they're so friendly. Always help you out. Not like the people in the States. I know. I was in the retail business for years. Retired at forty. You get to know what life's like in the business world. How long have you been here?"

"Three weeks." It was all Jack could do to answer. We were stunned. We had not seen an American tourist like this since London. Apparently, Jack's two words were his allotment; our gabby guest was off and running.

"We're going off to the post office at Kildonan and then out to the islands. Meeting friends from the States. They came up the coast in their boat. From Portland. Lovely people. We meet every year. It's been real nice talking with you. We'll be back in a week and will spend a few days here. We'll spend more time together then."

And they were gone. It was a pity, Jack thought, that they had a motorboat rather than a sailboat; with their own wind a sailboat would have gone with the speed of sound.

~~~

IT IS an Asian custom to call each year by the name of a certain animal, such as, the Year of the Monkey or the Year of the Dog. Our first summer at Kildonan could have been called the Year of the Mouse.

They were everywhere. At night we could hear them holding wild orgies in the attic; by day they moved insolently through the gardens as if they, not us, had taken over. They were completely immune to any fear, save fear of Bjorke, who promptly dispatched those he caught to the next world. We could walk right up to them and be totally snubbed: They would barely bother to look up from the tender vines which appeared to be their main food.

I have no particular affinity for mice but neither do I have any cartoonist's dread of them; and these were the cutest mice I have ever seen. They were various shades of gray, some tinged with a little brown, and their underbellies were white as were their feet. They had two great rabbit ears hilariously disproportionate to their body size. They were the common white-footed mouse, or deer mouse, and they were plaguing the entire Kildonan area.

Jack detested them. He sleeps like a cat and I as if in a temporary death. Their vigorous and noisy carousing in the attic all through the night meant no loss of sleep to me.

"They have some form of perverted field sports over the bedroom, calisthenics over the living room and military training and obstacle courses over the kitchen," he roared after one particularly bad night.

I was slightly dismayed when he said he or the mice had to go, but agreed something had to be done. Growling still, Jack went up into the loft and then into the attic where he found what looked like a bushel of poisoned wheat, fifty rusty mousetraps and an old five-gallon water trap. Vigorous with efficiency, he made out a list of required supplies for the *Lady Rose* to deliver next time it came into Kildonan.

On the next trip the *Lady Rose* sailed in with a supply of new traps and boxes of poison. I felt it should have been flying the skull and crossbones. As long as the mice did not come into my kitchen I believed they were harming nobody and that, in due course, they would go as swiftly as they had come. The poison was set out and the traps loaded with cheese. No results.

A few days later Jack came back from the *Lady Rose* with a couple of caramel candy bars. He felt sure these were just what the mice were looking for and he was right. Never before or since have we experienced such a ghastly night with the sound of those cute little creatures being executed throughout the house all night long—just because they liked caramel candy. By dawn I could hardly look at Jack, let alone speak to him, and by high noon we had reached the glaring stage. He was no happier about it than I.

"They've got to go somehow. Did you know they are eating all the insulation off the electrical outlets?"

I agreed they had to go; an hour later he was back triumphant. We could get rid of the hideously snapping traps and, although the mice would die, at least we would not have to share every rattle of their demise. Some local people had told Jack that the water trap was the best method of getting rid of them. You take a five-gallon bucket and remove the lid, then drill two holes on opposite sides about three inches below the rim. Next, smear a can with butter and cheese, run a rod through it and insert the can over the water where it is free to revolve. Then place a stick from the floor up the side of the bucket to the rod. The mouse smells the cheese, walks up the stick to the bucket's rim, sees the butter and cheese and leaps onto the revolving can, which slides him off into the water where he paddles until exhausted and finally drowns.

That night this fiendish contraption was hauled up into the attic. I took two glasses of sherry and went to bed in a mood of grand hauteur. I woke at dawn to find Jack slipping into bed beside me: "It didn't work," he said. "Thank God. What nightmares I would have had. All those pretty little gray things with their great funny ears drowning in our attic—just because they wanted a lick of butter and cheese."

It's strange how even mice can bring a couple together.

———～———

T HE weeks were passing with a peace and contentment we would not have dared hope for. By now we had become accustomed to the silence. It seemed to pluck all of the haste out of our lives and invest us with a quiet and productive energy. There was a lot of hard work to do—the dam was only one project—and some of it was backbreaking. To the side of the house, for instance, the old garden lay buried under a jungle of thorny bracken and second growth. It was a scratchy, tearing process to clear it but in a few days, almost without comment and with no complaints, we had it done. Freed from external pressures, we were slowly becoming our true energetic and creative selves. And although nothing was said, it was commonly understood that when the summer was over and we departed from our property it would have been beautified by our presence.

Despite the success of the summer and the growth that we were experiencing, my basic attitudes towards the cottage were unchanged. Our real home was in San Francisco and this was our summer home; there could be no thought of living here for many, many years. And yet . . . at times the thought of leaving and returning to the city seemed insane.

The truth was that, like many women of these times, I was struggling to find myself—not so much then as a writer but as a human being, a being freed of all the traditional roles that society had imposed upon me. The spontaneous imagery of "woman" in my mind paid tribute to the success of my childhood programing: Beauty, domesticity and dependency dominated while at the same time my daily life gave these images the back of my hand. Domesticity and the search for beauty bored me equally; to be dependent was anathema. My journalistic work repeatedly took me abroad and I felt as much at home in New Delhi, Tokyo, or Hong Kong as I did in San Francisco. And yet within me, and not too far under the surface, either, were mingled feelings of guilt and inadequacy because I had left my children for three weeks or was not home to cook my husband's dinner or did not know one end of a sewing machine from another. Women who had not been as successful as I were astonished when I would casually admit to these feelings. They had them, too, but they thought that miraculously success would wipe them out and leave not a tracing. How little they understood their own psychological castration.

By the very nature of my struggle I was compelled to return to the social body that had tried so hard to force me into bondage. Only by defying the oppressive forces in society could I hope to find my natural self. The freedom of Kildonan was empty to me. There was no way there that I could define and identify my freedom *as a woman*, of proving to myself that I had at last attained the freedom necessary to express my innermost self. While the isolation of Kildonan removed all false social constructs from my exterior life, constructs just as corrosive would remain within my psyche. I had to break out of the psychological prison created by society for women before I could make use of the greater freedom Kildonan offered me as a *human being*.

And so the peace and contentment that we had found at Kildonan made little impact on my determination to return here for each summer only. We did not discuss this. It was understood that we would leave, and Jack did not want to dwell on that day anymore than I.

August was a beautiful month and was marked by a stream of visitors. One couple was from Chicago. The husband had been attending, with his wife, a business conference in Seattle; both the children were in summer camp back East. When the conference was over they decided to visit us, a decision we welcomed, for we had known this couple for many years. Both were nature-lovers and keen on outdoor sports, so we decided to take them to Henderson Lake.

The southern tip of Henderson Lake, which is one of the larger lakes on Vancouver Island, is just over a mile away from the head of Uchucklesit Inlet, or, to put it another way, a mile from where we and the bears picked blackberries. As the elevation of the lake is only two or three feet above sea level, it is possible to travel by boat from the salt water of the inlet, to the pool and up a river to the lake.

Although not as large as California's Lake Tahoe, Henderson Lake is just as lovely. The water is turquoise-blue and crystal-clear to fifty feet, and gravel beaches ring the shores—beaches of stones so round and smooth that each seems to have been polished by hand. The trees on the slopes around the lake are massive. Giant cedar, fir, hemlock and balsam are the fruit of the annual rainfall of 263 inches, the highest recorded rainfall in Canada and perhaps the highest in North America, with the exception of some remote parts of southwestern Alaska. The timbered slopes sweep up to jagged mountain peaks which are permanently frosted with snow. One day we counted sixty-seven creeks and streams emptying into Henderson, many by a charming, if miniature, waterfall. Around these outlets we have seen deer and the small black bear that inhabit these parts.

It was a mild and balmy day when we took our Chicago friends into this paradise. They had been with us only three days but there was already a feeling of strain. This surprised us, for in the city we had always plenty to discuss. On the first day we had shown them around the property, on the second around the area a few miles in each direction, and on the third day we had planned nothing, believing they might like to soak up the beauty and solitude without activity. The day without activity seemed to have left them depressed, so we planned a picnic to Henderson Lake for the following noon.

We crossed the lake and found a whitened, gravelly beach scattered with old trees that had fallen down naturally decades ago and now had the patina of old silver. After lunch the husband sank into a reverie as he gazed at the opposite shore. How pleased we were that its mystery entranced him, too. He spoke: "The potential takes my breath away. You could leave one part of the shoreline just as it is. Over there you could level the timber, and with a double-lane highway around the lake you could build the most beautiful subdivision in North America. Gas stations, supermarkets, trailer parks, boat-launching ramps, and a dozen or more retirement villages. You could make millions."

"How about a motel over there?" asked Jack when he had recovered his equilibrium. "Over there where you plan to level it all. You could leave one tree standing and call it Lone Pine Motel."

Our Chicago friend gave him a quizzical look, thought about it and said: "Don't think that it isn't going to be done just as I said one day."

When they had left for the wilds of Chicago we thought a lot about our friends. We'd never entertained the notion that, with all their chatter about conservation and outdoor sports, they would not enjoy the natural beauty and solitude that our property had offered. In reality, they had both suffered intensely from it. To have heard them talk, one could have drawn no other conclusion but complete commitment to the natural outdoors. But what they loved in reality was not the snow, the mountains, the trees and the fresh air provided by their skiing, or the spumy delights of sailing; what they liked was the social life of the ski lodge or the yacht club, entrée to which was contingent on a show of outdoorsiness.

This incident caused us to recall our own experiences camping in California over the past twenty years, particularly in Yosemite Valley where, on a warm afternoon, the smog level due to camp fires and the population density per square foot is greater than in any Los Angeles suburb. Sites that could be reached only by foot three or four miles away were deserted.

We agreed that few people at any socio-economic level really like the untouched wilderness. They like a glimpse of it but with all the comforts of home—a paved parking space, flush toilets and television reception. The thought saddened us, for it implied that those who love nature in its untouched purity might be too few in number to stop the accelerating destruction of this continent.

EVERY so often one of our neighbors, Bob or Ethel Reynolds or Chrissie or Hugo Johnson, would ask us if we had found "the pad."

As I said earlier, the property had once served as a marine filling station and far above it, somewhere on the other side of the stream, was this foundation on which the oil tanks had once stood. One afternoon, close to the end of our stay, when the days were shortening and some of the leaves had already turned yellow, we set out to find it. We crossed the stream near the beach and, hacking our way through thick second growth, stumbled upon some wooden steps almost covered in ivy and succulents. We cleared them one at a time, edging up through brush, ivy, salal and small saplings, using our machetes to go an inch. For city types like us, limbered up though we were by the work already done, it was an almost overwhelming struggle. Jack and I were still struggling when one of the boys shouted: "I've found it! I've found the pad!"

When we reached it, it looked unreal, like the remains of a temple built by some early tribe and left to be swallowed up in the jungle. Only parts of the pad protruded. We tore away at the vines and salal and exposed a sheet of concrete forty feet long by sixteen feet wide and eighteen inches thick. It sat like a granite monument on the hillside, facing the inlet and dominating the old house and jetty far-removed below.

We were dumfounded by the discovery, at least Jack and I were. The boys were high with excitement and chattering like jaybirds. To us the finding and location of this pad was almost like a sign. The pad was a perfect foundation for a beautiful home. Here we could build cheaply and well, turn the mountainside into a riot of flowers, put a bridge across the river and later add a little teahouse to the side where the river splashed down into a moss-ringed pool. I saw it in a flash. It goes without saying that Jack, a born builder, saw it in even more perfect detail. We sat together on the edge of the concrete, our legs swinging over the small incline below, and he said quietly: "Wouldn't it be nice not to go back? To jump out of bed with joy in the morning and

not give a damn about how we looked or acting smart
or getting ahead? Not to have to commute or care about
what everyone else thinks? Just to be ourselves and enjoy
the experience of tasting life, real life. Wouldn't it be
wonderful?"

It was not a question but a wistful statement devoid
of any hope of sharing. And all the ambivalence in
my nature stirred. Oh, yes, it would be wonderful, I
thought, and this was followed by, it would be terrible.
I am a woman, ordained by nature for pretty, delicate
things, for a social life, to be seen and admired, not
buried away in a wilderness. My mind replied: You could
be free here. But my programing shouted back: Free like
a deer in the woods? While all my friends dine and dance
in splendor? Oh, don't be an ass, my brain responded
impatiently, for it did not like this other, false me. And
I turned to Jack and said aloud: "You could build a fine
home here."

He was surprised but ready. "I'd put the living room
here with a large stone fireplace. See the ducks by the
jetty? We could sit by the fire and read and watch
them play. A farmhouse-type kitchen. A couple of bedrooms upstairs. That's all we need."

It's all *you* need, the programed part of my mind
thought with a spurt of anger. It *is* all you need, Lisa,
the free part of me said: Here you will find all that you
wish to know and will become all that you wish to become.

We sat side by side for a long time in silence. I could
hear our sons yelling at each other high in the hills and
the distant sound of the dog barking. I noticed that Jack
was wearing the same old work sweater he had worn for
many years; there was something dear and comforting

about it. He turned to me: "You wouldn't do it, would you?"

"I can't see how it would work."

"Because you don't want it to work?"

"I didn't say that."

"I don't give a damn what you said. I want the truth."

So as best I could I gave it to him—not the truth, the real truth of my deep interior struggle—but easily understandable, easily articulated superficialities. I was not yet at a point where I could easily define and verbalize my struggles as a feminist. He would have understood—in fact, told me later even then he understood—but the difficulties inherent in finding my identity as a woman were so threatening and confused I could not spell them out. So I rambled on about children and social responsibility and what would happen if everyone dropped out and all that cant, and I didn't believe a word of it and neither did he. Finally I cried: "You'd be running away from life!"

"Quite the opposite," he said, "we'd be running towards life."

A<small>ND</small> so, two weeks after Crispin and Jonathan found the concrete pad, we packed up, locked the house and boat shed, and started the long journey back to San Francisco.

I was aware that Jack disliked living in San Francisco to the point of pain. It was not San Francisco as such that he rejected; his feelings would have been the same towards New York, Toronto, Tokyo or London. Every fiber of his being rejected city life just as every fiber responded to the isolated wilderness. A student of history for years and a voracious reader, he did not see our times, or his moment on the stage as being the most important period of history. The explosive events hurled at us every day in the city were seen by him in terms of a mosaic, as a fragment devoid of any meaning if not viewed in historical perspective.

During our brief time at Kildonan this perspective sharpened because the news coming across the radio had no impact on our lives. The current world could have been a radio play written by Orson Welles; the news conveyed no reality whereas the overview of historical events did. The happenings which are such a rewarding part of city life, if one lives one's life out in the actions of others, offered him nothing.

I knew this; but when the moment came for locking up, and carrying our baggage to the end of the dock and waiting for the *Lady Rose,* we told each other that, after all, we had planned to come for the summer only. We spoke rather awkwardly about our home in San Francisco, and the improvements we could make there, and our jobs. Once on the *Lady Rose* we went up to the ship's railings and watched a part of our life fade away. How impractical it would be to live here! How could we live? Where would the children go to school? Why, everyone had such dreams, but *you just couldn't do it.*

And so we went back.

Moby Dick was under the tree where we had left him three months earlier. He had turned brown under a quarter-inch coating of dust. We took him down to the gas station, where he drank his first gasoline in weeks and let forth with a great satisfied roar. With reluctance we bade goodbye to those we had met during the summer: Kay and John Monrufet, Dick McMinn, August Johansen, first mate of the *Lady Rose*—they were part of an experience that had marked us. Then we drove out of town, passed the motel, swung onto the highway, and Port Alberni and the valley disappeared.

After being dependent on one's feet for three months, traveling by automobile is comparable to flying. Forty miles an hour was thrilling; how wonderful had we been able to hold onto that sensation. But soon Jack's manhood was coming back as the soul of Moby Dick. Within fifty miles the other cars became as other people and we started pushing faster than was either necessary or rational. The expensive cars became important, the faster cars a challenge, the old jalopies objects of ridicule. Had we really thought that three months would undo forty years of conditioning? In the one hundred and forty miles between Port Alberni and Victoria, the reality of our Kildonan life was buried under the fruits of our programing in an industrial society.

Both Jack and I could feel the slow rise of pressures. What time did the ferry sail? Did we have time to get a new battery and gasoline? How much would it cost for the car and us? Would the tires last the thousand miles back to California? Would we be stopped for driving a vehicle that produced too much smoke? Where would we spend the night? Would we be able to get back by Sunday afternoon? Would we all become highway statistics?

When we reached Victoria we had a couple of hours before the ferry sailed for Port Angeles, in Washington State, at 5 A.M. So we did the only sensible thing—we parked the car and dozed. But not for long. We were awakened by a policeman who told us that sleeping in cars was not permitted, we would have to move along. We went to the ferry-building parking lot and, after some time, went through customs. There was obviously something very wrong with our image, for customs opened all our boxes and even checked the space behind the front seat. We were then asked where we had been and where we were going. Bjorke then had to show his papers indicating he had had the necessary rabies shots.

The ferry was nearly deserted. We settled the boys in the lounge and went to the coffee bar for a wake-up cup, but the waiter said he would not take Canadian money. We found enough American money for coffee but we might have been smarter had we shown less initiative, for the coffee and donuts that followed, untouched by human hands, were unfit for human stomachs. The donuts, blown out of some distant machine by the millions, were enveloped in plastic and tasted like cotton; the coffee, which came in styrofoam, tasted like nothing.

When the ferry bumped the Port Angeles slip, the car deck filled with blue fumes. The door was opened, the ramp lowered, with a metallic clang, and the vehicles slowly streamed out with stops and starts and angry expletives from impatient horns. We were going home.

The road from Port Angeles south is a single lane that runs in continuous curves. Not to be first is not to discover the horizon; not to be first is not to discover something new; not to be first is not to be important; not to be first is to follow a slow camper truck or trailer. So in time a pecking order is established. It is hardest for those who struggle, one car at a time, to get to the head, to be first, for there is no first. Someone is already there. Still they struggle to lead, just one more car, one more car today, one more car tomorrow, one more car forever. Surely, if they struggle hard enough, one day they will become the head of the line!

The towns passed one after another, each stamped out of the same maximum-profit machine: gas stations, root-beer stands, supermarkets and shopping centers, nationwide motels, more gas stations, and then another town.

"Good morning, shall I fill her up?"

Yes, fill her up and check the oil. Say, do you get much rain around here? But why bother asking the gas-station attendant, he doesn't know. He was in Texas last year and Chicago two years before that. Just give him cash or credit-card and take off.

It was not so long ago that a long automobile trip for all concerned was a social affair. The station attendant had a wealth of information about local climate, crops, politics and history. He was often the owner and knew everyone and everything in the locale because he went to school there and to church and belonged to one of the local fraternities. He may even have known someone you knew. In any case he was interested to hear where you were from, where you were going, how you liked the car you were driving, and who did you think was going to win the next national election or the World Series?

It was a small parochial climate that one ran into at each gas station and sometimes the pettiness was irritating. But it was a comfortable and comforting way of life, for in a small way you were somebody, and what you were doing and where you were going were of interest, often genuine interest, to another person hundreds of miles from home. And the outcome of this casual friendly involvement was a sense of belonging to a community even if one were a stranger. Now at every gas stop and restaurant, we tasted the fruit of change—we were all strangers in a strange land, a nation of wanderers knowing only our own families (and even then not well), and interested only in whether one is paying by cash or credit-card.

For some miles we had looked forward to visiting a small town in Washington where Jack had worked as a farm laborer following military service during the Second World War. It would be nice for Crispin to see where his father had spent a part of his life as a young man.

When Jack was previously there the highway ran through the town, but now a green sign over the freeway told us that the turnoff to the town was a quarter of a mile ahead. We pulled off at the turn but found no town, just a crossroad running in two directions. There was another sign pointing to the right. We turned, passed a mountain of wrecked automobiles and arrived at a root-beer stand. The town was getting close. The revolving signs of a service station, followed by the familiar logo of a national chain market came into view. We turned left and were in the center of town.

The old country-style department store was gone, taken over by a neon-lit shell filled with flaming fluorescent goods for teenagers. The store across the road handled all adult clothing—mass produced, cheap and destined to drown anyone's identity. The old hardware store had vanished, the salesman couldn't say when. He was from Portland and had sold shoes there—but then you didn't have to know anything about hardware to sell it. The nuts, bolts and tools were all wrapped and labeled in plastic bags, designed in New York and made in Columbus and Chicago. In fact, much of the hardware was now plastic.

We drifted out and headed a few miles down the road to the farm where Jack had once worked. We crossed the railway tracks and drove west for ten minutes, Jack all the while looking for a certain hill to the north. He found it, it had been shaved and bulldozed. A television tower was atop it, sticking out like a *banderilla* from the back of a dead bull.

When we reached the spot where the house, barn and bunkhouse had stood, we found ourselves looking at a shopping center, a drive-in movie and a junior college. It was only a day after leaving Kildonan; we were too tired and sad to say anything. The boys broke into a torrent of questions. Why had the farmers left? If they

lived in the city, what did they do there? Where did all
the cows and horses go? If you pour concrete onto farmland and cut off the sun, will grass ever grow there again?

We tried to give the boys answers that were both
optimistic and realistic. It wasn't easy. They were asking for hope, hope for their own future, and we wanted
to give it; but they were also asking for fact. While I
did my best, Jack went off to phone some families he had
known in this area. But they were all gone, their names
no longer in the directory. It had all passed—the town
and its people—in the space of two decades. And so we
moved back to the freeway and headed south.

In the long hours that followed little was said. The
boys dozed and Jack and I took turns driving. Sometimes we flicked on the car radio, but the sameness was
worse than the silence. The music, the language, the
format, the excited, pressurized torrent that character-
izes the voice of the deejay—all seemed to be by-products
of the same machine. It became very obvious that there
was no profit to be made in anything regional, for regional products are removed from the milking, manipula-
tive skills of Madison Avenue. Yet there is no virtue in
being a nation of two hundred million people identical
from coast to coast, as far as I can see. The distance
between Seattle and San Francisco would have taken us
through two or three countries in Europe. We would
have heard different languages and music, seen regional
architecture and some variety of clothing, and in this
way would have caught a glimpse of man's diversity,
versatility, the infinitude of the human spirit. What we
saw with our eyes and heard with our ears had a bland
sameness that would have done credit to a totalitarian
system.

By the time we were halfway through Oregon Bjorke was badly in need of a feed and a walk. We turned off the highway and parked in the lot of a large shopping center that contained a supermarket. It was Saturday and the complex was as frantic as a disturbed anthill.

At Kildonan, the night before the *Lady Rose* came in, we would sit by the fire and write up our grocery list. If it were the Tuesday visit of the *Lady Rose*, the groceries would come in on Thursday. If it were the Thursday visit, the groceries would come in on the following Tuesday. We would discuss the list at leisure. Should we order ice cream or wait until the following week? Maybe then we could treat ourselves to extras, like nuts and whipping cream? When we planned and waited for goodies like this they seemed to taste more delicious. Some might call this a hangover from the old Protestant ethic; perhaps. It does not alter the fact that the ice cream tasted better when it assumed the dimension of something special.

Now we moved into the store after our three months of ordering by mail and with all the scales of former shopping habits fallen from our eyes.

Dear heavens, were these The People? Was this the soul of a nation that I saw before me, dressed in shorts, with broad beams swaying to and fro between the ketchup and the cornflakes; these creatures with their hair wired into curlers as if enduring an electroencephalograph as they plod through the produce department; these creatures with bare feet, which they expose nowhere but in the bathroom and when they buy food; these creatures with soft stomach rolls and hard faces nibbling potato chips while they shop for frozen juice? These creatures were *immortal?*

Staggering under our shock we located the pet food, guided there by a sign similar to those seen at political conventions, only in this case bearing the name of the cat or dog food rather than the politician. Nine different types in boxes and plastic bags, and an equal number of choices in cans, confronted us. We had to choose, as Bjorke was not allowed in the store. In view of what *had* been allowed in we felt the discrimination was in Bjorke's favor.

Jack picked a plastic bag filled with "real meat" patties that were designed more for human-impulse buying than the taste and needs of a hungry animal; then, joining the line, we slowly edged forward. At the cashier's stand, Jack handed over the dog food and a dollar. Down a metal chute into a metal cup came the change and out from a metal box popped five savings stamps. Not a word was spoken. Jack couldn't stand it, so he cheerfully asked: "Miss, what are these stamps for?"

Chaos! It seemed that nobody had ever asked that question before. The whole world knew what those stamps were for. For crying out loud—this said with a pitying laugh—where had we been all these years?

Outside Jack said he had sacrificed thirty-five minutes of his life to buy a box of dog food and had felt entitled to say something. The dog had no sympathy with his sacrifice; he spat the patties out one at a time. We assumed the first one was bad and it took us some time to realize that there was nothing to go bad, the patty was as organically dead as a piece of plastic. Bjorke is usually the soul of tact but this day, reentering the concrete world, he likely felt stripped of all grace. Perhaps it was the combination of a long wait on an empty stomach, and four paws being burned by hot concrete. Whatever moved him, we felt his spit-out demonstration appropriate.

We set off once again over land that Jack had traveled twenty years earlier looking for work. He could not recognize a single landmark or town. In two decades Oregon's hundred-year history had been erased. As we drove Jack fought off a sense of confusion, a mounting feeling that perhaps he had not been here before, surely there would be something he could recognize if these were the same small towns where he had stayed, searching for work on the local farms. But he had been there before, the green name signs over the freeway assured him that he had. The name was all that remained.

As the miles passed we became increasingly aware of the faces in the automobiles moving towards us on the other half of the freeway. Over nine hundred cars and trucks passed us within an hour. We would pass more than 20,000 drivers between Kildonan and San Francisco, more people than our rural grandparents might have seen in a lifetime. To help pass the time and amuse the boys, we would speculate on the face rushing towards us, would it be sad, happy, intelligent, lonely, mean, would we like to meet the person the face belonged to? It turned out there were thousands of faces we would have liked to meet but, of course, we met none of them. As the hours passed, Jack and I noticed a qualitative difference between our age and all ages that had preceded it. We sensed a pollution that is much more of a threat to our existence than dirty skies and water and that is the *pollution of our concepts.*

Like most people, we were raised to believe that each

human being is unique and valuable. But day and night unceasingly this stream of humanity rushed towards us, this fragment of the overpopulated world, and it rushed towards us in a setting that gave brutal evidence of its existence—miles of farmland buried under the concrete of freeways, bridges, abutments, overpasses and underpasses. Living in a nation with one-twentieth the population density of India, our mobility exposed us to more people in a few hours than most Indians, the majority of whom live in rural areas, would ever see. It is not surprising then that, despite chaotic natural pollution, the Indian living in the most polluted conditions still sees himself as valuable and unique, a child of God, while our concept of man's value and uniqueness is rapidly corroding. Man appears to be able to adapt to his physical environment, but as yet nobody knows whether it will be possible to give back to him his human and historical dignity, once it has been corroded by evidence of his insignificance among the uncountable number of his own species.

There were many times when we would have liked to stop the car and speak to somebody—to have said "Godspeed" to another traveler. But such a spontaneous and human gesture was impossible, it invited death. As each automobile passed it subtly whittled away at our concept of our own importance. The only possible contact we could have with another driver would be a collision at a velocity of over one hundred miles an hour. I had once read that the census figures are rounded off to the nearest one hundred thousand, and it struck us that if the four of us were killed, it would not even change the statistics.

A SMALL incident occurred late one night as we followed the long downhill grade that runs from the Shasta
area of northern California to the lowlands of the central
valley.

Somewhere along that vast concrete strip we passed
a camper truck with a State Highway Patrol vehicle
parked by the side of the road. A little farther on, coming to the lighted green sign of an official rest area, we
pulled off for a breather.

The rest area looked like the parking lot of a bank
in an upper-middle-class suburban neighborhood—lined
parking stalls, islands with flowers and small trees, lawned
areas and painted trash bins. There were swings for
children and, of course, rest rooms, but no rest room for
poor, patient Bjorke. We let him out but there was nowhere for him to go. The area was fenced in and, like
the parking lot at the bank, had not been designed with
Bjorke in mind. With a pang of conscience we tied him
to the car with a short piece of rope and told the poor
fellow he would have to wait until we had left the area.

We were about to fall asleep when a vehicle pulled in
beside us. We recognized the camper truck that we had
passed on the highway. From a roaring monologue, de-
livered by the driver to his wife specifically, and anyone
else who happened to be within shouting distance, it ap-

peared they had stopped for the night somewhere along the highway, only to have the police descend on them instantly and tell them to get moving as they could stop to sleep only in one of the rest areas provided by the state.

It was easy to imagine what had happened. Like hundreds of thousands of other Americans, they had purchased a camper truck to "explore and discover" America, as the advertisements so seductively say. Now they were learning firsthand that not only had America already been explored and discovered, but that camper trucks had turned most of the "wilderness" highways into a crawling, bumper-to-bumper commuter-type nightmare. Like a hundred others unable to find a camping area that was not already clogged with explorers, they had finally pulled off the road for the night, only to be told they had to find an approved stopping place or keep moving.

"Remember that incident in Wyoming?" Jack asked.

I remembered it. We were staying at a ranch owned by friends in the Snake River area. One day a state policeman, an acquaintance of the owner, dropped by while out on patrol. He was a cartoon cop, overweight and with a phalliclike cannon hanging from a low-slung belt, which was strained trying to keep up his stomach. Our friend asked the officer what he was doing to keep busy. He replied that he was "keeping the tourists moving."

We commented that many had come a great distance and at a considerable expense to see this "frontier" region. Surely they had as much right to be in Wyoming as any resident citizen.

The officer went straight to the point. During the

tourist season there would be over a million of "um"
wanting to camp along the road. And every one of them
would need to defecate at least once a day. The state
had no means of handling the mountain of shit that would
result, therefore, they had to keep "um" moving. If they
could get in, they could go to the approved camping
grounds where there were facilities; otherwise, they just
had to wait.

So much for Marlboro country.

W E ARRIVED back in San Francisco early one morning,
crossing the Oakland Bay Bridge from Highway 50, red-
eyed and tired, the children asleep on either side of me.
Everything looked the same. A thin wisp of dead-white
fog trailed in past the Golden Gate, the hills of Marin
County faded into the blue of the Pacific, a few sailboats
dotted the harbor. The Embarcadero was like a ghost
town; the wharves that had once served the fleets of the
seven seas were deserted.

We swung south on the freeways that entangle the
suburbs; they, too, were deserted. Later that day there
was to be a ball game at Candlestick Park—this was the
quiet before the chaos. We sped along past billboards,
each with a message—where to fly and what airline,
what kind of whiskey to drink, how to show your class
by moving into Sunny Shingles development, how to find

happiness by purchasing a certain automobile. Then off
the freeway and past the Southern Pacific Railroad yards.
Old yellow buildings, half-fallen fences, piles of rusty
iron, roads of broken pavement and an air of disuse and
decay. What a monument to the industry that dominated
all phases of American life just forty years ago! Up the
hills and around the winding, unmade road that led to
our pretty house.

The boys were stirring. Were they dreaming they
were wandering up the mountainside with their great
bounding dog or swimming off the jetty in that crystal
water, or lying snug in their cabin while the raccoons
stole our blackberries? I gently woke them and told them
we were home. Jack said: "Speak for yourself."

It was a mistake to arrive home from Kildonan on a
Sunday and return to work the next day. We were both
tired but our tiredness was beyond anything physical.
Our spirits had been nourished for months on natural
beauty and personal freedom, but even I, who had wanted
to come back, felt I was crawling into a cage. I can only
guess at how Jack felt, for we both declined to discuss
it. Although we knew we were causing each other distress
we were powerless to alleviate it. It was no easy question
of my "freeing" Jack to go back to Kildonan, for he was
free to go when he chose, but what freedom is it for a
man to leave his wife and children? There could be no
thought of it, just as I could not bring the idea of pack-
ing up and leaving for the wilderness out of the realm of
dreaming and into the realm of a possible, even practical,
alternate style of life. It would require a subtle and continuing pressure to put my psyche into another space
where I could even consider it. This pressure was to come

not only out of the polluted environment, nor out of the increasing tensions in our marriage, but from within my own depths. We were in for a rough year.

The boys went back to school, I returned to the *San Francisco Examiner* and Jack returned to teaching.

I had worked at the *Examiner* for eight years and had many acquaintances and a few very close friends. Many of them stopped by on my first day back to remark on my tan, how well I looked, and ask what had I been doing. Invariably, they listened with sincere interest to the story of our summer odyssey, saying at the end: "That's just the sort of place we want. Are there any others like it?" They would shake their heads in near disbelief when I described the purity of the water, the beauty of the night's blackness, the depth of contentment possible in total silence. I was to repeat this story many times, finding in its repetition a growing nostalgia and an increasing ability to clarify and define my own feelings. With time, it was the intensity of others' interest and the pathos of their longing to get away to a similar place that helped precipitate in me not only a similar appreciation but a true understanding of the forces at work within Jack. What he wanted to do, millions of other men wanted to do, but he had the means of doing it.

He arrived home late from his first day back at teaching, looking drawn and gray and quiescently middle-class in the uniform I had so carefully selected for him —blue oxford button-down shirt, knit tie, gray slacks and tweed jacket. The children were already in bed and he went down to talk with them and kiss them goodnight. Still unaware of his unreconcilable depth of dislike for the city, I had tried to make our home appear especially

attractive and in doing so was living out some of the
worst aspects of my feminine programing. I was patheti-
cally employing, as so many women do, silver and damask
on a candle-lit dinner table to woo and seduce granite.
There was a fire lit in our Swedish fireplace; in the distant clear, cool night could be seen the lights of the
Oakland Bay Bridge.

We ate in silence. After dinner Jack told of his first
day back at teaching. It was like being in a twilight zone.
After class there was a prolonged teachers' meeting—
two hours of heated discussion on who would clean the
blackboards, the teachers or janitors. It was what they
did best, Jack growled—talk. He was firmly convinced
that few of them were capable of doing anything else,
that they craved the authority of the schoolroom and
could not compete normally in the outside world. Teaching was their only chance of gaining authority, and
questions of tenure and job protection devoured their
waking hours. How in God's name could a mind obsessed
by tenure cultivate the freedom of spirit necessary to
bring out the creativity of a child? Frightened, impotent
minds, that was the spiritual bank of the teaching pro-
fession! Spiritual virgins from whose aridity the mind
of youth is supposed to be fertilized! Jack was in prime
form.

"It wouldn't be so bad if the students were getting
some objective reality, such as physics or foreign languages. But nobody can ever ask for the bathroom in
French or describe what happens when a rock is thrown;
yet every one of my students is an expert on government
and politics. Our society doesn't demand that we learn
anything. Why should we? If you're a movie star, you

can play golf with the president and spout forth on any damn subject under the sun and be listened to with more respect than men who have devoted their lives to the subject. All a kid needs today to survive are psychological tools. What's important is the ability to bull one's way through dinner rapping about child psychology or Vietnam."

America is a machine-oriented society, not a people-oriented society: "It's a society built on physics rather than on humanity, and everything that needs to be done can be done by one percent of the population or by a computer and nobody has to be a fully developed twentieth-century human being to survive."

It just was not going to work! Here we were back two days and the frustrations that Jack was expressing were normally the end-of-the-school-year symptoms! It was as if the peace and contentment that we had stored within us at Kildonan was flowing away unchecked; as if its very nature could not stay within us in this environment. In the days that followed I tried to replenish my dwindling sense of inner harmony. I would take quiet moments and let my whole being dwell on one specific feature, such as the pale green crystal-clear water, or the sound of the rain on the inlet, or the sight of a cloud tangled in the trees. One night I sighed and said how beautiful it had been at Kildonan: "The tide would be in now and the sun setting. How busy all the little creatures must be now that we have left them in peace."

The words were out before I realized the possible effects.

"Let's go back, Mom," the boys said. "What's so great about living here?"

Afterwards I told Jack that it was obvious I also

missed Kildonan, that I, too, had been happy there: "But for a lifetime, that's something else. We can't afford to take the risk of finding out. We can barely get along now on $20,000 a year. What in heaven's name would we do in the wilderness?"

It was many weeks before Kildonan was mentioned again.

───⌣───

Oᴜʀ lives appeared to slip back into the old pattern. We left the house together in the morning, dropping the boys off at their schools, then going on to work. Bjorke was left outside on the patio, which overlooked the Bay. He would stand up on the patio fence as we left, great paws on the redwood and his face furrowed with sadness. Were it not for the bounding, unabashed welcome we received on our return, it would have been unbearable to leave him thus. Dear Bjorke! His unfailing daily exuberance on our return added immeasurably to our spirits that trying winter.

I must say that the career aspect of my life was most satisfying. As a reporter, and later as a columnist, I was involved in many of the tumultuous happenings of the middle and late sixties. Every week brought something destined to shake one's traditional values and beliefs—the free-speech movement at the University of California at Berkeley, open-heart surgery at Stanford

Medical Center, organ transplants at the U.C. Medical
Center, the growth and flowering of the flower children,
then the hippie movement in the Haight-Ashbury district, the discovery and widespread use of the psychedelic
drugs, the student movement, and the soul-searing black-
white police confrontations at San Francisco State College and elsewhere. Those of us in the news media were
in the thick of it. We were at the nerve ends of every
conflict and the pressures at times were almost intoler-
able.

As well as my work on the *Examiner*, I appeared as
part of a press panel on a medical-educational program
coming out of Oakland's Channel 2, KTVU. There were
also invitations to speak at many universities and colleges
about my visit to mainland China. This was work that I
particularly enjoyed, for a whole generation existed in
this most affluent society who knew nothing whatsoever
about one-fourth of the world's people.

Jack took a sincere pride in my career. There was
none of the resentment expressed by so many men when
their wives act as intelligent and independent beings.
When I was successful he glowed; when I failed, he
shared the disappointment. We had always acted as a
team. Our children never came back to an empty house,
either he or I was there. Sometimes I would be away for
two or three weeks in Asia; then he cooked dinner, took
the clothes to the laundry, saw that the boys did their
homework, cleaned house, and he did it all with both
pride and freedom while lesser males derided him.

There was a subtle change after we returned from
Kildonan. At first it was barely perceptible. As in all
close relationships it is often impossible to finger the

shifts and changes in the currents running between two people. Gradually, the shift in attitude became more definable, a growing casualness to some family project, then indifference to some specific need such as getting the drycleaning back or picking the car up at the garage. We were starting to play little hidden and hostile games we had not played before. Perhaps they are common enough in all marriages at times of stress but after so much warmth and sunlight they hurt disproportionately. We became at once critical and defensive. Long ago we had decided that a trained orangutan could make a perfect housewife. Jack had said a score of times that if he had wanted a perfect housekeeper, he would not have married me, as I had said I would not have married him had I wanted a man driven solely by material success. Now our capacity to ignore what we had both espoused for a decade and a half appeared total. Even the cat got into the act—*my* cat. She was ruining our expensive couch by sharpening her claws on the fabric! And as for poor old Bjorke, it was cruel to keep such a dog in the city, he was made for the country and perhaps we should look for another home for him!

We were a couple in anguish. Over the years we had analyzed and adjusted to many differences between us, certainly a normal procedure in marriage, but in our case complicated by the fact that I came from a bourgeois Australian family while Jack, whose hard-working family had migrated from the Canadian prairies during the flu epidemic of 1919, was from California. This process of adjustment had been painful at times, but we felt intensely that the life journey we were taking together was far more interesting, even nobler, as a result. Now,

the struggle to define Kildonan in relation to our marriage was creating a stress we had not experienced before.

For me the city was exciting—the meeting place of
the interesting and the successful, a place of life, new
ideas and beautiful things. Jack saw it as dirty, noisy,
the home of pawnshops, skidrow derelicts, crude girlie
shows for the lonely, employment offices for the unqualified, welfare offices for those left behind. The city meant
jail for the true losers and the home of the masses who
had no other alternative but to stay put. All forms of
competition, body and mind, were considered good by
those who had raised and taught me; all relationships
ultimately depended on who was the winner and who the
loser. One came to understand that some people "counted"
and some did not; the successful counted.

Nearly all traces of this curious perception of humanity were swept aside during my visit to China in 1965,
when I saw the need to destroy the old class structures,
which precluded human beings from being accepted for
their worth, for their contribution to society, no matter
how humble or menial that contribution might be. I had
not applied this need to my own American society, believing it to be possible in the new society of China but
impossible in the infinitely more complex American society.

During those winter months, however, my perceptions
started to shift and change. I had always thought highly
of success, of being a winner, not so much because I
cherished success, but rather because a certain indepen-
dence demanded defying those persons and forces in
society which would keep me in a secondary position be-

cause I was a woman. When I looked at the games that
were being played out daily at the *Examiner,* which was
no better or worse than any other office, and at the
fruits of this co-called success, my appetite for it dwindled.

I could not rid my mind of the contrast between the
stench and the grape-colored water of Port Alberni, and
the water of Uchucklesit Inlet, or the sight of a mountainside covered in tall timber and the devastation of a
logged area. To market century-old trees for last Sunday's paper, to design a new automobile that pollutes
the air or discover a new product whose wastes destroy
Lake Erie scarcely looked like success. And to be in a
position to do these wondrous things one had to perform
superbly in the caste system of superior and inferior,
practice treachery, flatter nits, and think dirty. The
social pages were filled with the envied activities of people who had made money from manufacturing pollu-
tants or destroying rural areas through real estate speculation. Academics who spread fear and division gained
instant national notoriety; politicians who spoke plati-
tudes and sidestepped commitment to solving social problems appeared to stay in power indefinitely.

Success no longer interested me; I understood the
game. If I were successful, it was going to be an accident,
not an end. I discussed this with Jack, as well as the fact
that I now understood that the city to him was repre-
sentative of all the horrors that mankind can impose
upon mankind and that what he longed for was sane and
good. It was good to say these things, to get rid of any
notion that I considered his needs neurotic or irrespon-
sible. Perhaps they were contrasted to society's demands

but then society was sick indeed. As these thoughts were
verbalized, the force, validity and beauty of his dreams
took on a new dimension. I no longer had to rationalize
his desire to return to the wilderness. Although it was
not for me, I saw this desire as proper and healthy.

As I began to speak about these things to friends,
cautiously at first and then more and more openly, I was
surprised to find an instant response. Many women told
of their husbands being obsessed by this dream—the
dream of freedom in the land of the free and the brave,
the dream of being their own boss, of starting a task
and being allowed to see it through to its end, of not
having to dress, look and speak for twelve hours a day
like actors playing before a critical audience. In confidence they spoke of their husbands' recurrent depres-
sions, irritability, moodiness and a melancholy that sometimes bordered on madness. I glimpsed a nation of men
caught in the wheels of the vast American dream machine
that consumed body and soul for $200 a week.

When one person in a relationship changes his position
important shifts follow. Once I understood Jack's position even though it was not identical to my own, and we
could discuss these matters confidently and calmly, the
question of whether we should go back to the wilderness
or stay in San Francisco lost its destructive impact.
After all, there was no big insoluble problem, just two
people with two children, a dog and a house in San Francisco and one in British Columbia. It was a matter of
choosing where we would live, and by any standards in
this world we were fortunate to have such a choice.

Jack and the boys had no doubt; it took a trip to
Los Angeles to help me make up my mind.

⌒ ⌒

Jack was born in Los Angeles; his parents brought him home from the hospital to a small weatherboard house that is now in the center of Watts. The family moved often. Like many Southern California families, their life was a search. In describing the many moves during his childhood, Jack says that whenever he gained the confidence to cross the street, walk to school and make friends the family moved.

One of these moves took the family close to the Baldwin estate. The Baldwins were one of the first families, other than Spanish, to build a home in the arid semi-desert that is now Los Angeles. In the summer of 1936, Jack inherited the fruit of their pioneering labors for his eight-year-old pleasure—four houses, both deserted, two barns, a lake surrounded by trees, gardens, paths, and a trail through the hills dotted with ancient oaks. Wild peacocks roamed the length of the estate, and so did Jack, playing in the barns and houses, fishing in the lake and hunting for peacock feathers.

A couple of times each year Tarzan and Cheetah would arrive with some elephants to make a movie. And once there was a great battle staged on the lake between two river boats, while at another time an airstrip was cut out of a small meadow and, while the planes took off and landed, Jack sat in the limb of a tree and watched.

When we went to Los Angeles on this particular trip we took the boys out to the old Baldwin estate, not expecting to find it intact, but hardly expecting to find it erased. Part of the gardens have been leveled for use as a parking lot and the rest is a county park. There is a fence around to keep little boys out, and an attendant to tell people that it was once a home. The lovely ancient oaks have been felled and houses now stand on the hill. As we declined to force on the boys the fact that when they are middle-aged nothing of their childhood will remain, we did not mention what we had *not* found. No point in rubbing their noses in the fact that their social lives were built on shifting sands. We let them believe in Santa Claus and the Easter Rabbit, so why not let them believe their schools, houses and streets would stay with them for the rest of their lives?

A multistory van and storage building rested on the buried foundation of the little hospital where Jack was born, and on the spot where he had received his first tricycle, on his fourth birthday, stood a highrise apartment building. The house from where he had first set out to school was under the San Pedro freeway, and the house in which he had learned to ride a bicycle was burned during the Watts riots. We could not stay around the Watts area long; we were intruders and unwanted, so we drove out to Santa Anita Avenue, where Jack had lived in his teens.

In those times people identified the avenue with: "You can't miss it. It's got two rows of large eucalyptus trees down the middle."

In the middle, covered with leaves and twigs, was a bridle path. From time to time the wind blew and the earthy deposits swept across the avenue and that is anathema to modern living. Leaves and twigs must be cleaned up and that costs money, so the beautiful old eucalypti were felled and the path paved.

We drove on to El Monte Boulevard. In Jack's childhood, when there were heavy rains, the wash emptied into the boulevard, closing it for days. The traffic was forced to go around. It was a wonderful time with a whole sea for battleships and sailors, for chucking in rocks and cans (but never bottles for they were sold for pennies to the junkman). When the roads were flooded a man named George came in an old truck and lit kerosene lamps to show that the water was too high to cross. The children helped him and sometimes blew them out when he had gone. Such days existed only in Jack's memory and in the memory of the others who once played there, for long ago the Army Corps of Engineers put a concrete ditch along the roadside and fenced it off with high steel.

In the days that followed, our trip assumed the aspect of a mobile inquiry. Everyone we met spoke of "home," but "home" was "back there"—in Iowa, Indiana, Oklahoma, New York or the South. That was where "the folks" lived. Grandpa was buried in the churchyard and three generations had been educated in the same schoolhouse. On the front lawn of the city hall were monuments from the Civil War, the Spanish-American War, World War I, World War II and the Korean War. They spoke of tree-lined streets, the swing on the front porch and of burning leaves in the street in the fall of the year. Why had they come here? For what purpose had they made Jack a stranger in his own hometown?

We kept driving but there was little to see. Not many years ago it was possible to take a streetcar to Sierra Madre and walk to the top of Mount Wilson. Nine hours' walking through the pine trees and shaded ferns in little canyons, past the Halfway House, where a drink and a visit were expected, and then one was on top of the coastal range looking out over the San Gabriel Valley, across the city of Los Angeles, past San Pedro Hills and out over the Pacific to Santa Catalina Island.

But everyone had to have a car, then two cars, then three—in richer families four and five. So the streetcars have gone, the mountains and Halfway House set aflame, and the San Gabriel Valley, the San Pedro Hills and the blue Pacific have disappeared from sight under a blanket of yellow-brown smog.

We drove south to Long Beach, where we had lived shortly after our marriage. Had there really been a beach there? Now a breakwater holds the sea back and the harbor has been successfully drilled for oil. In full possession of the ocean front, which in any healthy society should belong to the people, the oil companies made a gesture that verges on the pathological—they placed false fronts on the oil towers so they look like highrise buildings. Next to them on man-made islands they placed palm trees which, for all I know, might be plastic. The child who now comes to Long Beach has no warm sand between his toes nor a sparkling sea to bathe in; let him feast his eyes and soul on an oil derrick faced with a phony highrise building.

Wherever we went, whether to a restaurant or gas station or motel or store, we found ourselves caught like birds in a swirling migration, weaving, circling, all landing together but going nowhere. What were all these people searching for, what were they living for, why had they searched by the millions for a new place in which to live, and in so doing had created the third greatest migration of people in history? The first was the Christian Crusades, the second the migration to the New World, and the third is the continuing shift of people to the western coastal areas of North America. By their coming to California they destroyed what they came after, perhaps a more beautiful setting, a more exciting job, a less limited future. Maybe more than anything they felt they were escaping from loneliness, from the loneliness that is in the heart of millions in this country who are unwanted and unqualified, the millions who, being told they were created in the image and likeness of Almighty God, find themselves trapped in the unending role of debt-ridden consumer.

When we left Los Angeles, I knew Jack had made up his mind to return permanently to Kildonan the next summer. In my heart I knew I would go too but, for the time being, I chose to let this knowledge grow and strengthen within me so that I might be sure and comfortable with it.

~

WHEN we told our friends that we were moving to the wilderness of British Columbia they were aghast. My friends assured me I was not "cut out" for the wilderness. They hinted that I was being treated most shabbily and the more they hinted the more confident I grew in my decision. I was saying goodbye to many of them for the last time; a year later I was to be a different person, with different values, from a different world and with little in common with them other than goodwill and memories.

Fellow teachers suggested to Jack he was running away, that he wanted to get back to the "good old days." Chain-smoking and twitching, they hinted darkly that a man should be able to cope with modern society, that there was something wrong with the man who could not. We felt we had provided them with endless speculation at their miserable cocktail parties. The question uppermost in everyone's mind was: How will you live, where will you get your income? When we cheerfully replied that that question would be looked into after we got there, the normal reaction was to be affronted. We were jousting at the Protestant Ethic, the grout of modern society.

As for those who hinted that we were running away, that we felt insecure, we replied: "You're darn right. The world is doomed by nuclear bombs or bacterial warfare, the lakes are dying, the open spaces disappearing, the water no longer fit to drink, the air too unhealthy to breathe, or so the experts say, and that *does* make me kind of insecure. How about you?"

Were we running away from American society? Our feelings were not those of running away but going to. Had we owned land in Oregon or Washington State we would have gone there. It was an accident in one respect that our new life was to be over the border and into Canada, I might add a most happy accident.

We sold our lovely house at a loss; we had put more money into it than we could ever hope to get back. We took the loss in the spirit that we were making a great improvement in our lives and this was the price that had to be paid. The furniture was packed and shipped, the second car, a small foreign model, given away, good-byes were said and addresses exchanged, and once again we were on our way with Moby Dick, older and more gassy by a year and grunting under a swaying load, but ours forever! We didn't stop once to look back.

WHEN we arrived at our home all nature worked to give us a warm and gracious welcome. The inlet was sapphire-blue and flashing under a light breeze, which had the tall timber humming. The creek was splashing over the gray rocks as if we had never left, and the daisies by the power house and the pink and purple fuchsia were in full bloom. The honeysuckle was already dead on the trellised bower but the perfume was sweet, sweet enough to have the hummingbirds exploring the vines. The boardwalk under our feet, the overgrown patch of lawn with a tiny garden stream running through it, the old wooden steps onto the verandah—all seemed dear and familiar. Jack turned the keys on the two locks on the front door and said: "We're home now."

There had been no visitors in our nine months' absence except a few mice; everything was as we had left it. There was about the house a placidness, as if we humans had gone away, had our disagreements and now, with all that behind us, were returning to a house of peace, to a house whose very simplicity forbade entrance to disharmony. For a little while we all wandered around, in and out, touching, looking, exclaiming. The blackberry bushes between the house and cabin were thick with fruit ripening. We opened the cabin windows and doors, pulled back the curtains and let the sunshine in. Then we returned to the main house, swept and dusted, then set to putting away our San Francisco furniture.

The boat shed took a ton of books and two bedroom suites before making strange, straining noises. Into our bedroom in the old house we put most of the living-room furniture, making it difficult to get into bed at night and almost impossible to get out in the morning.

What should we do with our paintings and pictures? We decided to enjoy some of the pretty things that we owned, not in the future, but now. So to the collection of fishnets, corks and glass balls already in the living room we added two oil paintings of sailing ships, a Japanese wall screen, etchings from England and rubbings from the temples at Angkor Wat. Over the window I hung a wooden cowbell that I had bought for a quarter in Cambodia, and by the door we put a fall of flutelike bells from a Chinese temple that we had found in a Victoria antique store. By decorator standards the mood was that of madness; we felt quite comfortable in that mood. Two years earlier such a conglomeration would have made me as nervous as a cat. Now I limbered up on the outrage to such an extent that the horror of the pink-brick fireplace, the centerpiece in the scene, receded to the point where I stopped telling the dog to go stand in front of it.

~

O<small>NE</small> of our first projects was to make the clinker-built inboard seaworthy. Jack bought a blowtorch, and under a hot summer sun we took turns burning and scraping off the old paint and putting on a new coat. Once it was done, we turned out as a family to launch the yacht. But the miserable thing leaked. It leaked so much we were always sinking, crossing the inlet while bailing and barking back to the jetty, not only with water coming through the bottom but rain coming in the top.

Leo, down at the logging camp, wanted to buy it and offered $100. We shared our opinion with him that he was crazy, that the boat leaked like a fountain. No, he wanted it; he would give one hundred dollars for it and so we sold it to him. Later he sold it for twenty-five dollars and a bottle of whiskey. It changed hands again for fifty dollars and now lies sunken and forlorn at Green Cove. So much for our first project.

Our second project was somewhat more successful. Jack and the boys tore down the old power house and put a new one on the old site. They then rebuilt the water wheel and arranged the machinery so as to take advantage of the known laws of mechanics, a factor missing in the original layout.

Our third project was to be our biggest. As we had decided to build a new home on the concrete pad high up on the hill, it was necessary to put a bridge across the creek, and this compelled us to clear out a jungle of brush and salal as well as several fine young alders. Then the four of us hauled the lumber up the mountain on our backs while Bjorke supervised. Jack drilled holes into the sides of the smooth slate-gray crevasse, inserted steel pins and laid the first beams. Today we have a fine old-fashioned New England covered bridge about twenty feet long with a roof of cedar shingles.

Sometimes when I am standing on the bridge now, looking at the inlet far below our moss-covered pool or waterfall immediately under me, I find it hard to believe that we actually carried up the lumber on our backs. At times enthusiasm can be one's worst enemy. It would have been a comparatively simple matter to have strung a cable from the beach to a tree near the bridge's location, but by the time we thought of it the bridge was nearly finished.

As a matter of fact the bridge is still nearly finished after three years. But we tell ourselves that the few finishing touches that are needed can well wait until we have nothing better to do.

W<small>HILE</small> the bridge was being built preparatory to building a new house, the other aspects of our lives went on as before. We read to the boys a lot, listened to the radio or our high-fidelity stereo at night, wrote out our shopping lists and on Tuesday and Thursday went off to the Kildonan post office to collect our mail and groceries when the *Lady Rose* arrived.

We were, as before, subject to a great deal of attention from tourists. To stand on the post-office float as the *Lady Rose* docked was to bear the expectant gaze of fifty beaming faces and just as many cameras. At night we would wonder, sometimes with the boys pantomiming, about the remarks that would be made months later when these same tourists invited in their friends for slides or movies of their vacation trip; for as soon as the *Lady Rose* had docked, there would be a flood of questions: Did we live here? How did we get our groceries? What is the dog's name? Where did the children go to school? Is the fishing any good?

One day our two sons caused a mild panic among the passengers of the *Lady Rose*. I was over in Vancouver collecting material for a free-lance article—an absence that was to be repeated many times in the future as our financial resources gradually dwindled. Some time earlier we had ordered a secondhand stove from the city and now that I was away Jack had taken the opportunity to remodel the kitchen.

It so happened that while I was gone word came from the shippers that the stove was coming down on the *Lady Rose* the following Friday. Kildonan was not on the Friday schedule of stops, nor was it possible to divert from the schedule on that particular day.

On Thursday afternoon, Jack raced out into the inlet in his new aluminum outboard to meet the *Lady Rose*.

Shouting out to the bridge from his small bobbing boat, he told of the stove's impending arrival while tourists stared and cameras whirled. The captain said he would bring it into Kildonan the following Tuesday. No, Jack shouted, I would be home by then and he wanted the kitchen finished before I arrived. So it was decided that the *Lady Rose* would stop in mid-channel the following morning and lower the stove over the side "as long as you've got something we can put it on."

The next morning was foggy and cold. We had a heavy float made from logs and timbers, the one used to store the old inboard clinker boat the first year we were at Kildonan. The eighteen-horsepower aluminum outboard was tied to the back of the float, and two hours before the *Lady Rose* was due off the mouth of the Uchucklesit Inlet, Crispin, Jonathan and Bjorke set off, pushing the float slowly along with the boat.

By the time the boys were at the prearranged meeting point a light rain had begun to fall. From this spot in the middle of the Alberni Canal there is no sign of habitation in any direction, just mountains, trees and miles of remote coastline.

At the appointed hour the *Lady Rose* came into view, breaking through the rain and throbbing to a stop while the boys pushed the barge alongside. Then the stove was lowered onto it. Having completed the job, the boys edged the float away from the *Lady Rose*, which started up her engines and disappeared into the mist, her deckload of tourists in a ferment of alarm and curiosity, as we were to hear later from the ship's crew. All day they spoke of the two boys and their dog on the raft

bobbing on the water seemingly a million miles from any
sign of habitation. Did they have parents? Did they go
to school? What did they eat? Who did they play with?

The scenes in many homes in the months that followed
can well be imagined when, with the movie screen up on
the wall and friends in for coffee, the tale of their summer vacation was told—along with a spreading concern
for the two little boys and their great big dog alone on a
float with a stove in the middle of the wilderness.

The boys were not the only ones who provided diver-
sion for the tourists. Sometime during the summer, a
character who lives permanently in the Broken Island
group, who never goes to town and who must remain
nameless, told Captain John Monrufet that he needed two
pairs of long johns and would the captain please buy
them for him. John obliged, and for many weeks carried
the long johns up and down the canal waiting for his
customer to reappear. One foggy morning when the
Lady Rose was working her way through the islands
with the help of radar, Captain Monrufet picked up a
small blip.

The *Lady Rose* stopped and soon, from out of the
fog, a small wooden boat came alongside as the tourists
moved over to the rail to see what was happening.

"Hey John," the character shouted, "do you have my
damned underwear?"

A lower hatch was opened, a parcel handed through,
and standing up in his boat our friend held up the long
johns to full view. "No damn good, John. I wanted black
ones with buttons all the way down the front." With
that he threw the broken parcel through the hatch.

The long johns were returned and the correct style traveled aboard the ship for a week or two before the little wooden boat once again appeared out of the fog to pick up the acceptable merchandise. The charge for this personalized shopping service, including the freight, was one dollar!

———⌣———

During the middle of the summer, Jack received a letter from a former student asking if he could come and bring a friend.

Jack replied that he would be pleased to have him and his friend, but please, *please* let us know when they were coming, and please bring some milk, bread and a little meat. Jack explained, at some length, our difficulties regarding lack of refrigeration space and availability of fresh vegetables, for our flourishing vegetable garden had not yet come into existence.

One day when we were all so tired we could hardly stir, the student and his friend arrived, "absolutely starving" as they so succinctly described it, and without notice. They brought two cans of beans and a case of soda pop.

I think that's what you would call a view of the generation gap from the other side.

⌣

ONE day quite early in summer we were clearing brush on the side of a hill when we were startled by the flight of a grouse from some nearby bushes. We gave the grouse and its nest a wide berth and some time later were delighted to find it was sitting on a hatch of nine eggs. The nest was poor, however, built on sloping ground with little to hold the eggs securely. Jonathan was fascinated. When would the eggs hatch; what would the chicks look like; what did they eat? He had the insatiable appetite of a little city boy whose only intimate experience with wildlife had been watching television shows such as "Flipper" or "Walt Disney." It had seemed so easy there, the parents being an unending source of scientific knowledge and practical know-how. Now Jonathan turned to us with the full expectation that we would know all that human knowledge encompassed on the subject of grouse, whereas in fact we knew nothing and it would take us at least three weeks to get the information he required.

A few days later Jonathan burst into the house; five eggs had broken loose of the nest and rolled down the hill. We had always thought that birds by nature would build only to nature's perfection. Our experience with the grouse nest was just the first of several similar experiences in which we found that animals and birds, like people, do not always act prudently. There were smart birds and not-so-smart birds, and the universally perfect nest did not exist except in illustrations of children's books.

We took a dish and went up the hill and collected the runaway eggs. Then we took the eggs from the nest, scooped out the dirt, padded it with dry grass and twigs, placed low boards around it and replaced the eggs. A few hours later the grouse was back on her eggs and for the next two weeks Jonathan went up and down the hill like a Yo-yo. Finally he could contain himself no longer. Could a couple of eggs be taken from the nest and hatched from a light bulb as he had seen it done at school? We said no as this would mean that the water wheel would have to be kept running all night. We held this position for some two hours only, for why had we come to Kildonan if not to allow the boys to become involved with nature?

A small cardboard box was found under the house and after some experimentation with different sizes of light bulbs we found a combination that gave approximately the correct temperature. Four eggs were then taken gently from the nest and placed in the box. That night Jonathan marched into the living room carrying his sleeping bag. He had cut a small hole in the top of the box and covered it with clear plastic—a window to the world of nature. He put his sleeping bag on the floor and the box beside him. He was asleep in ten minutes and assured us in the morning that he had watched all night.

On the third night he noticed a small hole in one of the eggs and in the two hours that followed three live chicks were hatched. The fourth egg was no good and one of the three that hatched was imperfect and soon died; I am sorry to report that the pecking of the two healthy chicks contributed to it. Jonathan called his two chicks Henry and Alvin, for reasons unknown, and they flourished. For a while we kept them in the house, an arrangement that Bjorke did not care about as they kept walking over his frame as he slept before the fire.

In time they were moved to a large wooden box in the boat shed, the box being set up with a number of light bulbs to maintain the proper heat. It was quite a tricky little chore for Jack each evening to turn the lights off in the house a few at a time, turn the valve down on the water wheel, and then turn off more lights and more water until only the bulbs in the box were lit. In time Alvin and Henry graduated from the boat shed to a pen on the lawn.

One evening Jonathan had Alvin out for a walk when Alvin surprised us by taking wing and flying off to the forest at the side of the house. Despite the fact that his coloration was such that one could step on him during the day unawares, Jonathan, with a lantern in hand, wandered through the forest calling his name but without success. Later, when Jack and I were reading and the boys had long since gone to bed, Jonathan walked into the living room. A number of quiet tears had been shed but it seemed as if Alvin's return to the wilderness had been accepted. Without a word Jonathan took the Bible from the bookshelf and returned to his little room.

The next morning when Jack went out to turn on the power, Alvin was waiting on the front steps. Nothing has been said to this day, the Bible has long since been returned to the shelf, and Henry and Alvin are grand-parents by now, having been freed when they reached full growth.

———— ⁓ ————

THE alder leaves were turning red and a cold wind was starting to blow across the inlet early each afternoon. The salmon were coming into the inlet in great schools, bounding out of the water as if pursued, a rich horde making its way to the spawning ground at the inlet's head. Autumn was coming and it would soon be time for the boys to leave us.

As there was no local school—the old one-room school-house which still stood on the Reynolds' property had been closed a decade earlier when the rendering plant died—three alternatives faced us. The boys could take all their schooling through correspondence, they could go into Port Alberni and board with a family and the provincial government would pay part of the cost, or they could go to private (called in Canada "indepen-dent") boarding schools. Without much hesitation we chose the last alternative. The idea of boarding schools is foreign to most Americans but I had gone to one and considered it a very happy time in my life, still maintaining friendships that were made there. We felt

it would be a lonely life for our boys to stay at home
and do their lessons by correspondence, nor could we see
leaving California and then putting them into such a
polluted spot as Port Alberni. There were four affirma-
tive votes for the schools we visited and decided on. Because of their age difference, they could not attend the
same school and, in fact, showed a remarkably indepen-
dent attitude about being together at school anyway.
Crispin's school, Brentwood College, was at Mill Bay
and Jonathan's at Cliffside, at Shawnigan Lake, both
located about thirty miles north of Victoria, the capital
city of British Columbia. Both schools offered excellent
academic programs as well as sailing, swimming, skiing,
Rugby, soccer and a wide variety of hobbies, the standards
being such that these schools attract students from all
over the world.

WE HAD decided to wait for the money from our San
Francisco house before ordering the material for the
new house. So we were into September before the lumber
was ordered and by this time both boys were at school.

Jack purchased all his material from a Port Alberni
lumberyard. He tried to get a discount by buying all the
lumber he needed at one time but it was to no avail. As

a matter of fact, we ended up paying more for lumber in Port Alberni than we would have paid anywhere else, even though Port Alberni is little more than an extension of one large mill. Worse, much of the lumber offered was of poor quality; according to the locals, the better lumber is shipped out of the country.

We made arrangements to bring all the lumber in on one trip, and the two captain owners of the *Lady Rose*, John Monrufet and Richard McMinn, agreed to a special sailing to Kildonan. So one Saturday late in September Jack left me in the custody of a delighted Bjorke and went into town where he helped the crew load just over ten thousand board feet of lumber onto the decks of the *Lady Rose*. The job was finished late in the afternoon, and Jack with Captain Monrufet and his lovely wife, Kay, sailed for Kildonan.

In the late afternoon the *Lady Rose* came through Chaputs Pass looking like an old Pacific coast lumber steamer. Later we heard that many pictures had been taken of the loading operation and without doubt one or two of these will one day end up on the walls of the Provincial or Maritime Museum, depicting the last remnant of an era.

It was dark by the time the *Lady Rose* tied up at our dock, and the men decided to unload the following morning.

The next morning brought a dark overcast sky and a steady rain. It also brought out Robert Reynolds, our neighbor, with a much-appreciated offer of help. Sunday was generally a day of rest for Bob, a retired tugboat captain, but on this occasion he managed to draw a parallel between the ass falling into the well and the need to get the ship unloaded.

The first step was to bring our raft, sixteen by twenty feet, alongside the *Lady Rose*. The lumber was then lowered by ship's crane onto the raft until it was nearly two feet under water. This left more than half the lumber on the ship.

The next step was to lower a great part of the remainder into the water and float it ashore where it was picked out and stacked piece by piece above the high-water level.

This still left a mass of lumber on board. Jack hesitated to put it on the fifty-year-old jetty. On the other hand, John Monrufet expounded on what he called "the snowflake theory." He said that many times he had seen structures hold up tons of snow because the load was piled on flake by flake, no one flake heavy enough to bring down the structure. And if the remaining lumber were unloaded piece by piece gently onto the jetty, there would be no danger.

Late in the afternoon the ship sailed for Port Alberni. The amount of lumber on the float, the jetty and the beach shocked the eye. How on earth was this going to be turned into a mountainside home? When I asked, Jack replied: "By the snowflake method, one board at a time."

I was in the kitchen and did not hear the crash. But I could hear the human reverberations: "Fifty feet of jetty gone. Right in the middle. I was standing there when I felt a sensation as if I were going down in an elevator. Everything so sodden and old there was nothing to break. It was as if it were made of butter and the sun had shone and it melted."

All I could see on the sunken middle was a pile of two-by-fours nearly down to the level of the water.

"What are you going to do now?"

"Remove the two-by-fours by the snowflake method. One at a time." He stood there silently. As I went back into the house I could hear him muttering: "Snowflake method, indeed!"

———~———

A FEW days later after Jack had cleared the lumber off the beach, he set out to bring in the load that still was tied to the float. He tied our new aluminum outboard behind it and was moving towards the beach for off-loading when the tide pushed the float towards the jetty. The heavily loaded float was going too fast to stop. Horrified, Jack sat in the outboard and watched as it rammed full tilt into one of the pilings. The piling was knocked out of place and another section of the jetty gave way. Commented Jack in a mingling of annoyance and satisfaction: "Well, at least it didn't happen by the snowflake theory."

It was obvious that the whole jetty was decayed with dry rot. On our Schedule of Building and Repairs it was marked down for total replacement to take place in summer, 1970. Until then we had to contend with a jetty that looked like an accordian and, at times, sounded like one.

———— ‿ ————

THE days melted one into the other. There were no great highs and lows as we had known them in the city. There were no battles of personalities at teachers' meetings, no jockeying for top position in newspaper articles, or television interviews. No interior victories or defeats; no agonizing post-mortems as to what we might have done, said or thought; no meeting our neighbors or fellow men as rivals, competitors with a knife at our throats; no meeting with friends and acquaintances imprisoned in mutual masks of distrust and loneliness. No outside authority dominating the hours of our day, telling us to do this or that and make sure it's ready on time.

All we did was *experience*. We experienced silence, a silence that only the forces of nature could break—the wind brushing against the trees, or the shrieks of the sea gulls over the water, or the thunder of the creek against the rocks as the stream burgeoned with the increasing rains. We experienced darkness, a velvety primordial darkness; one looked to the moon or the stars for light. When we shut off our hydro-power, we stumbled body against body within our cottage like the blind. We experienced elemental cold when we arose and shared with cavemen the lust for heat. We huddled over our stove, rubbing our hands and turning our bodies, sighing with pleasure, and then went out into the cold.

We wore clothes that protected our bodies from cold and injury. To outsiders we would have looked grotesquely amusing; we neither noticed nor cared. Occasionally, we would come unexpectedly one on the other, or be hauling a piece of lumber together and, seeing each other with fresh eyes, would start to laugh and end up collapsed sitting in the mud or on a carpet of cedar needles, laughing not in derision but in joy. We were very aware of what we had almost missed.

I did what I could but I can't pretend to have done much of the building. Despite our move, I had a series of writing commitments that had to be fulfilled, and we were delighted to have them, for our expenses were heavy and our capital diminishing. Yet, forced absences, at first back to San Francisco and later Vancouver, did nothing to decrease our mutual sense of being in command of our bodies and our lives. Each time I returned it was with a growing sense that I was coming home, home where I was finding, and would find ever increasingly, the deepest of satisfactions and creative fulfillment.

Once home I threw myself into the pursuit of helping Jack. He had built a cable line from the middle of the jetty up over the stream and up the side of the hill to the pad. On the pad he had constructed a wooden winch. He would load the lengths of lumber onto the cable line and I would start the muscle-wracking process of hauling it up. Standing there in the wind and the rain, soaked to the skin, our hands blistered and our shoulders aching, we learned more than we could have by reading fifty books dealing with the realities of pioneer life. How false is the image projected by most history books and entertainment, particularly television. Nobody in his right mind would willingly return to that period: Getting up in a cold house, lighting a fire and waiting for its heat to cook some breakfast, dressing for the day's work in the cold and then leaving a warm house that will be like an icebox upon returning—soaked and shivering—five or six hours later, cutting wood, washing from a bucket of warm water heated on the stove, cooking the dinner meat in the fireplace because the wood consumption was too high to keep both the fireplace and the kitchen stove burning, washing dishes in the tin bucket, later using the same tin bucket for the laundry.

We decidedly did not want to be pioneers or go back to those times. And yet it was through experiencing many of the elements of those times that we found our- selves. There were some mornings when we gave up; hear- ing the wind or looking at the rain we said to heck with it, stoked the fire and stayed indoors. But we found to our surprise that our bodies had begun to assert them- selves. At first it was as if they knew our wills were weak and would readily respond if a protest against the cold or wet was sent up. Yet with time, it was as if the body gained a deep contentment from a task performed and could accept with full pleasure the rest, warmth and sustenance it received only after that task was satis- factorily fulfilled. The body seemed to become subservi- ent, but harmoniously so, to the beauty of the environ- ment, to our quiet contemplation of the meaning of life.

We were constantly learning new things. For instance, one of our endless needs was for firewood. Scores of logs, looking as if they would supply sufficient firewood for a year, float past our jetty every month. It took more trial, error and effort than we would care to recall before we knew what we were doing in the firewood department. We found out that most of the logs that float by are cedar, hemlock, balsam and, from time to time, spruce, but that fir is the best. No Presto logs ever flowed by! Cedar burns like paper and continually pops and cracks while giving off little heat. Hemlock will not burn unless its combustion is supported by other wood and unless where it has had a chance to dry out, seemingly from the beginning of time. We also burned a lot of spruce at the beginning. It isn't too bad for firewood, but now that we can tell it from other logs we no longer use it. Burning balsam is like trying to burn a wet rag.

Today, when a fir log floats by, Jack or one of the boys hurries out in the boat and tows it in. At high tide we float it in as close to the house as possible, cut it into "biscuits" about sixteen inches long, and then later split them for firewood. Jack says after four years he can now smell a fir log when it burns and is no longer surprised by a fire that neither sounds nor burns like a breakfast cereal.

This constant learning of new things was a major part of our expanding in consciousness; it was combined with many changes. There was the alteration in time that I mentioned earlier. Our outside activities were dominated by the availability of light, by the rising and setting of the sun. If a log had to be brought in off the inlet at high tide, and high tide was at 2 A.M., then it was the tides and the moon that set our sleeping and awakening. In allowing natural forces to determine our concept of time, we found a new lightness, an easy capacity to sleep and awake. We no longer needed eight and nine hours sleep at a stretch, although that is how much sleep we

normally had. But if we had to break this pattern, the
break was in harmony with the pattern of our lives.

All this—the experience of living in harmony with
nature, the shedding of false imagery through our clothes
and possessions, the meeting of neighbors and fellow men
as friends not competitors, the daily physical acts of
hauling lumber, scrambling up the mountainside, split-
ting wood—thrust us into a new consciousness of whole-
ness. It was not so much that we stood still and sloughed
off our old lives, old attitudes and old ingrained habits
of thought and action; it was more as if we had sped
forward or stepped up into a different world in which
our old life did not really matter, for it was as if it had
never existed.

WE DECIDED to call our property "Seekah Landing,"
seekah being an Indian word meaning, roughly, a calm
place for a boat to pass through.

There is only one disappointment at Seekah Landing
and that is the comparative lack of animal life. Part of
this is due to my own inadequate knowledge; were I more
sensitive to the habits and habitat of wildlife perhaps my
waiting and watching would not be so fruitless. And no
doubt the presence of Bjorke keeps many animals away
who might otherwise visit us.

Still, I suppose I write this as one spoiled by what

many people would regard as a feast of natural sights. We do see black bears from time to time scrounging for food along the beach at low tide. And twice we have come close to them as we have crossed the inlet in our boat, their black heads just out of the water as they swam across the inlet or from the mainland to an off-shore island. There are signs in the forest at the back of the house that bears are our neighbors but we are yet to see one there. As I climb the hills alone a lot, it is perhaps just as well, for although these bears are not normally aggressive, they do attack like all animals if frightened and cornered.

The closest deer we have seen have been at the head of the inlet and although there are cougars in the hills, we have neither seen nor heard them but have often come across their droppings on the logging road. Some game officers who have lived in British Columbia for many years have not seen the cougar free, although they have heard his shrill scream from time to time. Unless maddened by hunger or weakened by age, the cougar will not come near the dwellings of humans. In a very recent tragedy, a twelve-year-old boy was killed by a cougar after the lad had unwittingly stumbled into the cougar's den. Undoubtedly this tragedy will lend impetus to the image of the cougar as a vicious and predatory beast best annihilated by those who develop their ego strength by doing such things. The cougar, in fact, asks only to be left alone. I bear no gratitude to the great white hunters who have deprived me of any chance of seeing one of these most exquisite cats in its natural habitat.

We do have an abundance of raccoon, mink and otter. Sometimes we leave a couple of fish heads on the jetty just for the pleasure of hearing these little creatures come out of the water and woods to argue in high-pitched screams about whom the fish heads belong to. And often we are visited by seals. They go by the jetty, look curiously at us and then go down, apparently satisfied not to be seen again, for they have the capacity to stay down for twenty minutes or so at a stretch.

One night I had an experience that taught me the true meaning of the fear of the Lord. I was over in the cabin writing, the boys were asleep and Jack was reading. It was deathly silent. Then, as if it were two feet away from my head, came this strange and gross sigh. I froze, expecting to find a bear looking over my shoulder. I turned slowly but the cabin was empty. Plucking up my courage I pushed my face against the glass; it was like looking into a bottle of ink. Had I imagined it? I left the cabin and stepped outside. There was nothing there. And then the great sibilant swish came out of the darkness again. By now I was on the jetty and shouting: "A whale, a whale, there's a whale in our inlet!"

Jack came running. One great soulful sigh, actually the whale breathing and blowing, and then silence. He must have been almost on our beach, although in the darkness we did not even catch a glimpse of him.

The next day Fred Cootes, one of the oldest residents of the Indian reserve, told us that in his youth the number of whales in the inlet made it dangerous to venture far out in a small boat, and that during the salmon spawning season, the salmon came in such numbers that the waters all but boiled as the sea lions followed, a feasting army on the rampage.

As long as we see an occasional deer or a bear, or have the chance of hearing the long-drawn-out breathing of the whale, we are satisfied. If I express disappointment at the lack of animal life, it is simply because I wish they were friendlier and would visit us more often.

WE AWAITED the Christmas season with particular joy, for the boys were coming home for a month's stay. Dressed in long gray flannel suits, their school scarves trailing around their necks and almost to their knees, they seemed to have grown a foot since fall. Bjorke didn't stop bounding for two full days.

The boys were astonished at the work that had been done on the new house. Somehow its presence seemed to be part of our pleasure in the coming Christmas. It stood high on the side of the hill, a frame outlining a large kitchen, a still larger living room on the first floor, two bedrooms and a bathroom on the second floor. Both floors have been studded, the walls shiplapped, and the roof sheathed and shaked. The exterior walls were to be cedar, shaked on the top half, with one-by-twelve-inch vertical board and bat on the lower half.

Jack had made a deal with some of the men at the nearby logging camp to cut and split the cedar shakes. As they went home only on the weekends and so had

extra time during the week, it gave them an opportunity
to earn additional money and gave us the chance to get
a good hand-split shake at a reasonable price.

The arrangement had its disadvantages in that Jack
had to go to the camp by boat, tie the shakes in bundles,
carry the bundles to the boat, load the bundles onto our
boat, boat home, unload the bundles, carry them to the
bottom of the cableway, tie them four bundles at a time
to the wheeled cable cart, and then, if I were not there,
walk up the hill to the new house, crank the spool 286
times, and then untie the bundles.

It was in the middle of this operation that the boys
came home from school, and once again we understood
what having a family meant to the pioneers. The boys
went to work and, by the time the Christmas vacation
was over, we had made fifty-six trips to the logging camp
and hauled over four hundred bundles of shakes to the
house.

While this activity was going on, we were looking
forward to Christmas, each in his own way, for it was
going to be much different from any that we had had.
We knew it was going to be quiet. We knew it had to be
a planned Christmas in that there could be no last-minute
shopping rush. It was a time that demanded each of us
to focus solely on each other.

When Christmas came, it was a delightful surprise.
Devoid of any commercial aspects, or the noise of radio
or television or urban life, it was a pleasure that was
most simple. We cut our Christmas tree from our own
land and made ornaments from odds and ends of colored
paper and aluminum foil. The lights on the tree were

powered by electricity from the stream that ran outside our house.

Two days after Christmas, Kay and John Monrufet came down on the *Lady Rose* for an overnight stay, tying up to our float and the tumbling-down jetty. At night a soft rain and mist gave an unusual proportion to the ship, the lights from the deck and portholes casting strange patterns on the gently moving waters and the Canadian flag flapping from the sternpole. It was a pleasure to look down past the boat shed and the power house, along the old jetty, and see the *Lady Rose* looking, with its lights in the darkness, like the *Queen Mary*. It gave one a sense of owning a seaport or of ruling a small independent community in some far-off land.

———◦———

THE process of learning to live in the wilderness continued.

Over the Christmas holidays Crispin and the Monrufet's son, George, went fowl shooting and returned with two ducks called goldeneyes. We had been assured by all that they were very good to eat, particularly if they were marinated properly. So the day after the *Lady Rose* sailed back into the world, our share of the hunting was put into the oven.

Long before it was ready, I tossed the bird, the pot

and all the goodies cooking with it out the back door and into a new snow bank. Had it remained even a few minutes longer we would have been forced to evacuate the house, so foul is the smell. Even when it had cooled the dog would do nothing but sniff it from a distance.

There were feelings of guilt all around that we had killed once-living flesh and not vindicated this kill by turning it into food. It was a mistake of ignorance.

To this day we still hear that well-prepared goldeneyes are fit for the table of a king. But then the pages of history are full of mad kings.

That was our first and last attempt to live off the country.

＊＊＊

Shortly after Christmas, just before the boys returned to school, the weather suddenly turned cold. It started to snow, the temperature fell and kept falling and at the end of two weeks there were small, round, saucer-shaped pieces of ice floating in the inlet. As a boy Jack had devoured the adventures of explorers such as Byrd, Perry and Scott, and it was with great excitement that we were called out to look at the phenomenon called "pancake ice."

As the days passed, each one, two or three degrees colder than the last, the boys took to skating and playing on the hard new ice along the shore. By the time they had returned to school, the expected two inches of snow had risen to two feet and the inlet was fast icing over. Each day as Jack and I—he far more than I—worked on the new house we could see less and less water.

One day, while working on the balconies, Jack happened to glance up and see Bjorke's 140-pound frame galloping across the ice towards the mid-channel island as if the ice were concrete. Jack froze; if he yelled, Bjorke would return home at a similar happy gallop with the increased possibility of breaking through the ice. So Jack called one word: "Shame!" It must have rebounded over the inlet like the firing of a cannon, for suddenly Bjorke skidded in his tracks, looked over his shoulder and came back in a crouched position step by step, tail between his legs. Later, Jack checked the ice with a pick. It was nearly four inches thick and would have supported a truck.

"Darn dog knew it all the time," said Jack.

Day after day the temperature dropped. The snow kept falling. I had several lecture commitments on the East Coast of the United States that would keep me away for nearly a month, commitments that had been contracted for a year or so earlier. Jack was in one sense pleased to see me go, since for many, many years he had wanted to spend some time alone. And now, with these near Arctic conditions, the snow in great white drifts around the house, piled high on the jetty, smothering the float, and the *Lady Rose* grinding her way in, shoving and smashing the ice to reach the post office, it seemed a perfect time to be alone.

In recounting what happened during this white and frozen month of silence and aloneness, Jack says that so

keen was he to experience being truly alone, he regretted
the fact that the *Lady Rose* entered the inlet twice a
week. All his life had been spent in a social, urban environment playing the role of husband, father, employee,
teacher, neighbor or just as a person showing an acceptable social front while riding the bus. He wanted
to find out what he was like when stripped of the neces-
sity of role-playing.

The days were short, the air frozen, the nights long
and black. He rose in silence, got into stiff, cold work
clothes, and spent the day in a silence that was broken
only by the snuffling of the dog or the muffled thunder
of some great old tree far away heaving over in old age.

After a few days Jack remembered there was someone
at the logging camp who wanted to learn about electrical
circuits. As the man stayed in camp over the weekends,
Jack found himself down there the first weekend with a
deal. If the logger would cook Sunday dinner, Jack would
teach him about electrical circuits. After two weeks Jack
was taking trips to the logging camp one or two times a
week, standing with his back to the warm stove, talking,
talking about nothing. On the long, dark, cold and generally wet trip home in an open boat, sometimes skidding
over the top of ice blocks, he wished he had more will
power. The conversation, the company, was not worth
that long, cold, wet trip.

By month's end, in that world that was short and white
by day, long and black by night, Jack had learned
two things about himself—and perhaps about many
who are raised in an urban, social environment. He
liked being alone yet he dreaded being alone. Being alone
exposed him to his own primitive self. While one part of

him drew sustenance from the primordial silence and darkness, his programed urban soul became increasingly tense and frayed. The squeaking of the old house, something falling or shifting on the jetty, strange noises at night started to take on a new and nerve-wracking dimension. When the humming Pelton wheel changed its rhythm, Jack would jump up to see who was coming in a boat, although he fully realized no one was coming. The longer alone, the more often he found himself shining the flashlight out of the window to see who might be there. While working outdoors every day he looked forward to his hot bath at night. Now he could no longer enjoy it with any real peace. No sooner would he get into the tub than he would hear someone coming. Rushing through his bath, he would stand and listen, only to find that the water wheel had changed its hum, and on the dark porch and along the wide expanse of wooden boardwalk and jetty, the flashlight could pick up no trace of any life, animal or human, in the thick carpeting of snow.

It was an experience the like of which he would not wish to endure ever again. Prior to becoming a schoolteacher, Jack had worked as a mechanical engineer for twelve years; he was a man concerned with hard fact, cold reason and realities. Yet a month of almost absolute silence and aloneness had penetrated every layer of training and reason and shown him clearly how close to primitive man we twentieth-century humans are.

When I returned home, we talked about it at length, and came to see something that we should have seen before perhaps, so obvious was it now. That in our relationship we had disallowed mystery. We had tried to relate and live without permitting arbitrary and irrational impulses. By wanting to get to really "know" each other, we had attempted to remove by rationalization everything that was hidden and unique. And by reducing everything to a rational explanation, to a sharply honed definition, we had denied the existence of vast, unmapped territories within ourselves.

With this recognition came a further and a greater freedom and we started to practice it at once. Nearly two years earlier during our first summer we had taken the first steps by sleeping and waking when we chose. From this we had graduated to new freedoms in dress and play and physical activity. But now we moved to the greatest freedom two beings who live together can experience—the freedom to say what you are really thinking and feeling rather than what you should be thinking and feeling. This is the fountain of youth. To be free to respond spontaneously and authentically to whatever the stimulus, is to *know* that you are alive, breathing, unique in some way and of value and importance in nature's scheme of things. This knowledge is not the outcome of any rational process; it *is*, it quietly asserts itself in every inch of our fiber.

We started to use this freedom in simple ways, for, after all, we were leading simple lives. Everything became a means by which we could exercise our freedom, not necessarily in getting what we wanted but rather in the full, uninhibited expression of our true selves. Jack might want to listen to Beethoven, whereas I might have had my mind on the Clancey Brothers. We would both express our preferences and maybe have some of both, or it might turn out to be of less importance to one than the other. Or Jack

might want coffee for lunch whereas I preferred tea;
rather than hedging and playing polite games we said
what we wanted, then took it from there. No more of
thinking one thing and saying another, whether it be
choosing the seeds for the vegetable garden, handling one
of the children's problems or answering a letter.

We found that once we had expressed ourselves we no
longer cared nearly as much about the object of our
choice. It was the expression that was critical to our sense
of well-being, not the imposition of our individual tastes
on each other. To show ourselves to each other with
choices and moods and feelings and yearnings that could
not be explained rationally, and to know that the exposed self was accepted completely as a unique being,
that was our new-found freedom.

We stumbled upon aspects of our relationship that
had always existed but which, in our success-syndrome
rat-race city life, we had rejected. We found that we
amused each other in a deep and kind way, that some
of the characteristics that most irritated before had a
whimsical and unique charm in our new setting and our
new freedom. A simple example. When we had lived in
the city Jack had disliked dressing up; it was a cause of
occasional words between us. Now I could watch Jack
skimming down the inlet in his open boat, wearing his
great wide-brimmed Australian hat and his huge poncho
flying behind him like a madman's cape and *feel* that it
was great.

Another understanding came out of Jack's winter
month, frozen and alone, that very few men and women
raised in the city could survive psychologically in the
wilderness today. No matter how much man craves the

purity and peace of life in the wilderness, it is an experience that few can cope with, let alone act creatively
in. Devoid as one is of all social contact and any trace of
competition, the interior motivation necessary to get one
working and creating in such isolation must be all-con-
suming, almost violent in its force. The wilderness offers
no solution to the masses of people who feel that life is
being choked out of them in the city, nor does it offer
a practical solution to the problems of society itself. The
solutions to the problems of society on the whole must
come out of society itself.

———— ⌣ ————

F ROM the very beginning—I suppose from that moment nearly two summers earlier when the boys found the
pad and Jack and I sat there on that warm summer's day
trying to see into the future—Jack had visions of a house
with floor-to-ceiling windows across the front, and himself sitting in the living room in a leather chair, book in
hand, a fire in the hearth, and a view of the stream, inlet
and hills. So when the house reached the stage that
windows were required, he ordered six sheets of glass,
four by seven feet.

I remember the day they arrived, two large wooden
cases on the float and the *Lady Rose* sailing away on
the inlet. Jack had not handled glass before. How was

he to get these sheets up to the new house? Gingerly, he opened one case and, although he knew what was there, he looked appalled at the sight of those three double sheets.

The only gloves he had were fur-lined, not the best for handling sheets of glass.

"Listen," I said, "before you pick it up, hadn't you better give it some serious thought?"

"No point in giving it any thought," he shouted back from the float. "I've no information to think about."

With that he picked up the sheet as one would pick up a sheet of plasterboard, carried it up the gangway and started up the jetty. He was halfway to the cable line when the wind struck roughly across the water. It hit the sheet of glass, turned Jack around twice and sent him dancing, like a ballerina, with his precious cargo up the jetty. Then the wind dropped as quickly as it had come.

Jack had built a special wooden frame to carry the glass up the cableway to the new house. Crank by crank on the winch, it was jerked up the hill and slowly, kicking a foot of snow out of our way, we unloaded it and carefully laid it against the verandah. It was at this point that I left and went back to the house. I felt this was Jack's project, I could contribute little—besides, the suspense was unbearable.

Later that evening, Jack told me what had happened. Shortly after I left, the wind started up again. In order to climb onto the verandah and haul the glass up, it was necessary to release his hold on the glass for a few minutes, but he had nothing to tie it in place. Placing the sheet at a good lean, Jack waited for a low wind and then rushed onto the verandah. One short strong gust, and the sheet stood vertical; he caught it with split-second timing. Then he pulled it to the verandah and raised it to the first window.

The sheet did not fit. With a pounding heart he tried the next window frame, and then each in turn. The sheet was too big!

It took all day to get the six panes up to the new house—they were all too big by one-half inch.

All that night Jack pondered over the problem. He had had no experience whatsoever with cutting glass, but felt intuitively that to cut one-half inch off the edge of a seven-foot sheet was a task he was not equal to. The early morning found him in the living room with volume eleven of the *Encyclopaedia Britannica.* Ours is the 1910 edition but Jack had little fear of a subsequent advance in glass-cutting technology. And he was right, for the glass-cutters described looked like the first tool man had made after leaving the Stone Age.

Up in the new house, he lay the first sheet of glass on the floor, put a straightedge where he wanted to cut, and made the scribe for the cutter. He then put his fingers in place as the directions showed and pushed. Nothing happened. He tried again. The glass would not break. Frustrated and disappointed, and just plain angry with himself, he took a pair of pliers, grabbed the edge of the pane, and twisted. A piece broke off up to the scribe line. He broke off a second piece, an inch long. It worked! He spent the day there, crouched on the floor, chipping away at the edges like a chipmunk on a nut. In two days the windows were all in place and without a break. A job done each day in countless cities, but to us a triumph!

Wᴴɪʟᴇ the building of the house went on month after month, there were certain domestic chores that had to be done. One was the laundry.

When we sold our home in San Francisco and moved north, we left behind a new washing machine and dryer, as the electricity produced by the water wheel was not sufficient to run a dryer. So we left the twin appliances and used the washing machine left behind by the previous owner of Seekah Landing.

This machine was an old wringer model. Three rubber cups about six inches in diameter were mounted to a center post that moved up and down about one foot with each stroke. No doubt when the machine was new and equipped with an electric motor that controlled the speed, it might have done a tolerable job of washing. By 1968 it was a different story. The electric motor had been re- moved and a small Pelton-type water wheel had been installed in its place.

On wash days we would push the machine out of the boat shed onto the jetty. Because of the work involved we tended to save our washing until the boys were home for weekend breaks. Once the machine was on the jetty we formed a bucket brigade, running hot water from the bathroom up in the house down to the jetty. The clothes were then put in, soap added, the garden hose connected to the water wheel and the Kildonan fresh-air laundry was in business.

Soon we would be doubled up with laughter, for in that beautiful setting of mountains, trees and the blue waters of the inlet, the machine would take on a life of its own. Throwing out hot water and suds all over the jetty, the machine would jump up and down and take short, bouncing steps along the boardwalk. When we were all sufficiently covered with soap and water, and the clothes in the machine in tight balls, we knew the washing was done. After some months of soaking and unraveling, we took the old machine out for a ride to where it now rests under 500 feet of water. We had no qualms about dumping in this manner, as oceanographers say that a certain amount of junk like this makes an excellent protective area for fish to breed and the fry to hide and develop.

Now we needed another machine, really *needed* it, which is different from purchasing a manufactured item because of advertising or social pressure. Knowing that the beauty of Kildonan, and all the world, can be saved only when people stop purchasing machines they do not need, and make do with what they already have or what can be restored with a small amount of maintenance, Jack went into town and visited the Salvation Army and the Goodwill thrift stores where there were scores of good used machines for sale.

He found one for twenty dollars. It must be twenty-five years old but it washes. It does not get the clothes whiter than white or cleaner than clean or lint-free, but it does wash. After we have washed in soap flakes, never detergents, and Jack and I have hung the clothes on the line, surrounded by all that loveliness, a little lint in a shirt pocket does not seem much of a tragedy.

We can have whiter than white, cleaner than clean, and pockets that are lint-free—or we can have beauty. An oversimplification perhaps, but the making of this type of choice by millions of us is a start toward solving the pollution problem.

When we began to think seriously about a cook stove for the new house, we concluded that a modern gas range would be out of harmony with our new life-style. Furthermore, it would be frightfully expensive to operate, since it would have to be fueled by "rock gas," the local name for butane or propane gas. If rock gas could be purchased in large quantities, it would be reasonably economical, but safety restrictions imposed by the Department of Transport meant that the *Lady Rose* could not carry a container larger than one hundred pounds. To buy in such a small amount would be too expensive for year-round use.

Jack had the audacity to consider a wood-burning stove, but very briefly. The thought of cutting wood for the next fifty years charmed him no more than the vision of standing over it for fifty years charmed me.

During the summer, we took an excursion to Bamfield on the *Lady Rose* and met an interesting Vancouver couple on holiday with their two sons. They invited us to have dinner with them the next time we were in the city and we accepted. Their home was a fine old house in Vancouver's oldest residential area. In the kitchen they had an English coal-burning stove called an Aga. Al-

though smaller than the standard kitchen range, it
weighs just under one thousand pounds. It is insulated
throughout with fuller's earth, and has two hinged lids
on the enamel top that drop down to cover the burners
when not in use. There's no heat loss and a small scoop
of coal lasts twenty-four hours.

The spirit of detachment from the desire for material
possessions, which we appeared to have attained at Kildonan, evaporated at the sight of this magnificent stove.
Jack was in torment. To own an Aga was comparable to
owning one's own train. Where could we find one? We
were told not to bother writing to the manufacturer in
England, as letters from "Colonials" were not answered.
Since the stove cost nearly $1,000, our only hope of own-
ing one lay in finding a secondhand one. And so the
great west-coast Aga hunt was on. Appliance dealers
were of no help. They had long lists of those waiting for
a used Aga.

At last we found one, the last homeless Aga in Vancouver.
It was in an old shed in a yard containing the remains of
hundreds of refrigerators that had died during the last
twenty years and were still awaiting burial. For $75 a
path was cleared and five men helped Jack load the
stove onto a rented truck. He took off in triumph for
Port Alberni where he met with, "I didn't think they
made them anymore," and "You're not going to take
that to Seekah Landing?" and "How will you get that
thing up the hill?"

Within two days the Aga was setting on our float at
Kildonan. There was no possibility of getting it up the
hill intact, so Jack took it apart, removing in the process
twelve cubic feet of fuller's earth and placing it in

plastic bags. Fuller's earth is like the finest of face powders, and by the time the dismantling was finished the whole world appeared to be covered in a fine white dust. One by one the thirty major parts were pulled up to the new house by cable and winch.

Jack has had the two burner lids copperplated and the stove, built to outlive the British Empire, has been reassembled. We now have but two things to do: Find a supply of coal, and discourage guests from making comments that end up with, "But the Aga Khan."

BECAUSE of the house's position on the side of the hill, and the fact that it was being built mainly by one person, the architectural possibilities were greatly restricted. But within these possibilities, Jack wanted the house to be an expression of our personalities—I thought a rather risky proposition. That expression included two large fireplaces, one in the living room and one in the main bedroom, with a rough rock face and a stone hearth raised well above floor level.

Before the winter snows, we had collected a load of large marble rocks from one of the outlying islands. These sea-washed stones, some pitted with holes as if drummed by a pestle for years, made a lovely face for the fireplaces but we still needed stones for the hearth. Remembering the beach at Vernon Bay with its masses of smooth round stones of pale grays running to near purple, Jack set off with Bjorke to gather a load. I remained behind. If he failed to return, I could always summon help. If we both went and failed to return, our absence could have passed unnoticed for days.

It is quite a desolate trip to Vernon Bay in the early spring, for the air is cold and the water freezing. When Jack reached the bay he noticed a small surf on the beach, which should have warned him to turn back. He made the landing without difficulty but had trouble keeping the boat from broaching on the beach while he gathered rocks.

Finally he had the load and was pushing the boat stern first from the beach when two opposing forces met head on—an extra-large wave and a 140-pound dog. Bjorke, thinking he was being left behind, came over the bow, swamped the rock-laden boat, and it half sank off the beach of Vernon Bay.

Jack had planned his arrival at the bay under rising tide so that the rockladen boat setting on the beach would be lifted without effort by the incoming tide. But now the boat was submerged, the tide beginning to rise, Jack soaked to the skin and twenty miles from home and not a human being other than me between him and oblivion.

Plunging into the cold water, he worked like crazy unloading the rocks that it had taken him hours to put in, battling the temptation to throw most of the stones at the dog. Finally, with all the rocks back on the beach, Jack could bail out the boat and pull it back onto the beach to reload.

This time Jack made sure the dog was a quarter mile down the beach when he finally shoved off. A safe distance out, he whistled to Bjorke, who swam out to the boat and was hauled in, a process rather like landing an elephant seal. It was a long, cold ride home for both of them.

Scanning the opening of the inlet with binoculars, I heard the outboard motor long before I could pick them up in the fading light. When I saw them coming, I filled the tub, stoked the fire and put on the kettle.

The cold has long since been forgotten and the stones, looking as plump and as round as a flock of gray pigeons, make a beautiful hearth.

⌣

Now that the warmer weather is here and the house nearly finished, it is time for us to think about building a new float. The old float is beginning to sink like a ship that has sprung a hairbreadth leak, and the cables and chains that hold it in place are rusting through. Soon, unless we wish to arrive at Seekah Landing combat-marine-style, we must act.

Floats are usually made of three or four large logs laid side by side. Beams are drifted into place across the logs, a drift being almost any type of large nail or piece of old scrap iron that will serve the purpose. Rough planking is then nailed across the beams. Cedar is usually used but any combination of woods will do in a pinch, particularly if the makings of the float are being acquired by beachcombing.

Yet from the moment the float is finished, it starts to sink. The cells of wood fiber fill with water and weeks of hard labor start imperceptibly on their slow journey to the bottom of the sea. The process, of course, takes some years but it is speeded by a diabolical agent commonly called the teredo.

The teredo is not a Spanish bull but a wormlike, soft-bodied animal which is a bivalve mollusk, a member of the same group as the clam and oyster. Teredos range up to three feet in length and three-quarters of an inch in diameter.

From the day the floats strike the water as a log, the teredos have staked their claim. The bottom of a ship can be painted or sheathed with copper but for a rough log float neither of these methods is practical.

A little research brought to light a method described in *Handbook 21*, Department of Recreation and Conservation, British Columbia Provincial Museum. Underwater explosions, says the book, are an excellent means of controlling teredos. Not being trained in underwater demolition, and wishing to retain a distance between us and the Royal Canadian Mounted Police, we have rejected the gunpowder approach.

There are other problems to be considered. Once the new float has been built the next problem will be to keep it in place. With a fourteen-foot tidal range in a twenty-four-hour period, it is easy to make the cable chains too loose or too tight. If they are too tight, they wear out, if too loose the tide pushes and loosens the float at will. If there is a ramp down to the float from the jetty, as in our case, there is a constant problem of alignment, even though the bottom of the ramp has wheels. These are common problems around any harbor, but where the crew is comprised of a maximum number of four who are amateurs from the foreman down, they loom like mountains.

Once the float is finished and secured into place, we will face another problem—where to get some old automobile tires to affix as bumpers for the protection of boats. In urban areas, tires are a pollutant—littered along roads, thrown into gullies, dumped into the bay or left in the bushes of a city park. But at Kildonan old tires for floats must be shipped from town. Kildonan must be one of the few places left in the Western world where old tires are hard to get.

And then what to do with the old float? In the old days we could have turned it loose to drift off into the ocean. But today, with an increasing number of plastic boats and amateur captains appearing in the inlet, a nearly submerged float weighing tons is as dangerous as a reef. Nor, with our newly acquired antipollution conscience, could we turn it loose to drift onto a beach. It has no salvage value, it cannot be sold to a junk dealer or abandoned on a city street. It will not burn and it is too big to bury on our land. Having an old float is rather like having an old Cadillac that you can't give away. But at least this junk will eventually return to organic matter.

⌒

THE disposition of the old float is not our sole problem.

One morning, while sitting at the breakfast table, through the living-room window Crispin saw a dark object hurtle down from high behind the house onto the roof of the boat shed. We all ran to the window and had a fleeting glimpse of a large bald eagle flying low over the shore with an object clutched in its talons. It could only be one of Jonathan's pigeons.

Jonathan had been given two pairs the previous Christmas; they are prolific reproducers, and in a few months there were ten. We all considered these pretty creatures to be a lovely addition to Seekah Landing. This particular morning all ten were sitting on the boat-shed roof enjoying the morning sun, when they were spotted by the bald eagle out looking for prey. The older ones, more sensitive to the danger of being a sitting target, were in flight by the time of attack, but the younger ones did not move and so gave the eagle a choice. He picked a bright blue and white, the first young born at Kildonan.

The pigeons scattered and it was not until late that afternoon that the last one returned, a dovelike bird of a light and soft brown, also a young one. Its neck was deeply gashed and it seemed that the eagle had nearly had two. Jonathan took the loss stoically and somewhat philosophically. Now the pigeons are not let out unless one of us stands guard, for twice a day the eagle and its mate pass by to check out the breakfast situation.

For all of us it was a personal experience of the violence of nature. There had always been a clear danger to our Siamese cat, Katherine. We felt it would be only a matter of time before an eagle took her, so she found a loving home at the Monrufets'. We had felt that the pigeons, being so much less domesticated, could withstand nature's violent ways, but it was not so.

We have two alternatives apart from giving them occasional furtive flights. We can keep them safely locked up or we can let them lead a natural life with the threat of cruel slaughter descending from the sky.

〜

I*t* is a fine morning in spring, crisp but full of warm promises. The house is now near completion, reconstruction of The Dam of Family Patience has started, the power plant has been rebuilt so that it will be good for a hundred years, the boat shed has been reroofed, and the rebuilding of the jetty is under way. This week we will turn over the old vegetable garden in front of the cabin and replant; the soil is rich and productive.

In living as we have for the past two years we have found ourselves—and spent most of our money! Months ago we faced the fact that we could not go on living forever without some regular income. As Jack can build and create a place of beauty from this overwhelming wilderness, while researching subject matter that we hope one day soon to turn into a book, and since I have a fair earning capacity as a writer, we decided to switch traditional roles. We would work as a team, Jack building, and I writing features for the *Vancouver Sun*. We would do this until all the landscaping and building was complete and we were freer, as our sons grew older, of the need for the high income which their education demanded. Or we would simply do it for as long as we enjoyed it, which might be two years or twenty years. I research my work in Vancouver and do as much writing as possible at Seekah Landing.

We made the switch simply and naturally. I go back to my home in the wilds at every opportunity. This spring we will plant a garden of potatoes, beans, peas, radishes, lettuce and spinach, and I will take some of this back with me to the city as well as the fruit of our inlet, such as salmon or cod or abalone. There are naturally times when we are both moved by a deep desire to be together at Seekah Landing, yet our new-found contentment suffers no loss by our temporary partings. The freedom we have found has loosened us forever from all traditional concepts and has freed us to move and flow with ease as life demands.

For the time being, neither of us can think of a more growth-producing situation than the one we now enjoy with each of us having a domicile yet sharing our family home. On the brink of middle age we are finding growth, excitement and fascination in a twenty-year marriage. We find enormous pleasure in coming together in need and interest rather than in a sea of daily chores and mundane habits. We are enjoying each other so much in this new life-style that even when we are freed from producing the high income that is now imperative, perhaps we will still keep our two domiciles while maintaining one home. Who knows? That is the beauty of our new life— we do not know, and it no longer worries us that we do not know.

We both have a fundamental commitment to experience life. Jack experiences it best through a reading of history and a grappling with the forces of nature, while I experience it best through some interaction with other human beings in a variety of life situations. The joyous spin-off from our life in the wilds is that we not only accept this fundamental difference in our personalities but find it an endless source of fascination. We now understand that we live in many worlds. Freedom is the ability to live multiple lives at many different levels. Freedom is the state of mind that is open to and integrates a historical perspective with new ideas, a sense of tragedy with a delight in play, an awareness of death with a spontaneous reaction to life, a love of nature and an appreciation for man-made sights and sounds, a love of familiar places and a thirst for the new, a need for physical activity with a longing for the quiet of meditation.

RECENTLY, a sad event occurred, the consequences of which left us with a clear, strong hope that while we all might not be able to find a place like Kildonan, we can find a state of mind like Kildonan.

Not far from our place, at the head of the inlet, is a small Indian village. The Indians are the Uchucklesit people and the inlet bears their tribal name although it is generally referred to as Kildonan.

The village is a single line of wooden houses facing the inlet and built just above high water on the gravel beach. This beach was made by the waves of southeast winds blowing up the inlet during the winter months. Just opposite the village is the mouth of the Henderson River. The location of the village offers a good beach for launching small boats, and the proximity of the river offers a rich source of salmon during the spawning season, factors which no doubt determined the location by the first inhabitants.

There is no history of these people and what little official information exists is often unreliable. One elderly resident speaks of a raid by another tribe about the time of the coming of the whites in which most of the women and children were killed or carried off. Prior to this raid the village was large and prosperous, but it never recovered from this incident. At one time the Uchucklesits may have numbered two hundred and fifty but today there are only about forty in the band, most of whom are living in cities and towns both in Canada and the United States. At the present time there are four families, with a total population of about seven people, scattered among the nine houses that make up the village.

Percy Jackson lives alone. He is an elderly man with a sweet gentleness that comes with age and with an understanding of man's relationship to nature. Percy broke his foot some years ago. It never healed properly and gives him much pain, forcing him to walk with a crutch. He cuts his own firewood and takes care of his many cats and dog. He seldom misses the *Lady Rose* at the post office, though it is a good two-mile row each way in his dugout canoe.

Ella Jackson, Percy's sister-in-law, also lives alone. She is a silver-haired lady who reflects all the natural beauty of the indigenous people who once lived across the face of North America. Ella makes her living by weaving baskets from shore grass. As the grass used for weaving is found along the open coast, Mrs. Jackson on occasion takes the *Lady Rose* to Bamfield, where she spends a few days gathering her raw material along the shore; then she returns home, dries it out and weaves a variety of striking Indian designs into various-shaped baskets.

Ella does not speak English and is part of an old world that has nearly passed from view. There are few Ellas left just as there are few Kildonans. She is a perfect manifestation of human dignity and grace, and when she dies the world will be less for her passing.

A third family, made up of an elderly couple and their grown son, a commercial fisherman, lives at the other end of the village. They were the first family to have electric power and, because of a quirk of nature, have the only location suitable for television reception. The television antenna looks incongruous in this village with its old houses on the beach and boats pulled up just beyond high water. Not that there should not be any television—for in such a remote area it has more meaning than in a large city with other forms of amusement—but the laws

of nature that shaped the trees seem to be at great odds
with the laws of physics that shaped the television antenna.

The fourth family was that of Kelly Cootes and his
wife, Daisy.

Kelly was a magnificent-looking man, big and tall
with striking features, and an intelligence to match the
strength in his face. There was a disquieting superiority
about him that was never dispelled by his friendly and
courteous manner. He always had time for conversation,
greatly preferring to socialize than submit to the tedious
regimentation of life.

Kelly was fifty and had been a commercial fisherman
for most of those years. When we first met him at the
Kildonan post office he owned a small trolling boat, called
the *M-R*. His hope had always been to get a larger boat.
He spoke of this often, stating that the *M-R* was too
small to fish the "big bank," the shallow bar some twenty
miles off the west coast of Vancouver Island at the entrance of Barkley Sound. It was a matter of the sea being
too big and the boat being too small.

Not long ago Kelly got his new boat, a troller just
short of fifty feet in length. It was purchased in Victoria
and Kelly brought it up the coast to Kildonan. He was
proud of his boat as only men who make their living
from a hostile world like the sea can be. There was one
feature of the boat he did not like, and that was its
gasoline engine. Because of the danger of fire, he planned
to replace it with a diesel engine if the next season was
a good one.

Those plans are no more.

Late last fall, Kelly was at Bamfield selling a few fish.

It was late in the season but he had not caught and sold sufficient fish to enable him to draw unemployment insurance during the closed winter season. So he was making a last effort to fill his quota.

After selling his fish that day he moved the boat to the gas dock to refuel. He filled up the tanks and then went below to adjust an oil heater that he used to warm the boat during the cold weather. A moment later there was an explosion, a flash fire and in seconds the boat sank below the surface, taking Kelly with it. The next day a son-in-law dove for Kelly, and his body was taken to Port Alberni.

The place of burial was the village cemetery.

Robert Reynolds, our neighbor, picked us up about two o'clock and we rode together in his boat to the village for the internment service. It started to rain just before Bob came by and Jack remarked, as we climbed into the boat, that he had never seen it rain so hard.

After the two-mile trip to the village we tied up Bob's boat to a float some distance from Kelly's house and walked through the village to the float in front of his house.

To walk through a village like this is to walk through its past and present. For, unlike the work of modern man, which is done miles from his home, here the canoe building, basket weaving or berry collecting, and all the preparations for fishing are done at home. And as there are no public utilities, all the problems of collecting firewood and storing a supply of fuel are visible to the eye. Since there is no heavy equipment to deal with a house that collapses from age it is left there, for to remove it by hand is a monumental task. When a fishing boat is forty years old, no longer seaworthy and leaks so much water it would sink if left tied to a float, it must be beached if it is going to be used as salvage. This was the scene in the village the day of Kelly's funeral—an old house in the last stages of collapse, a few large firewood logs tied on the beach above high water, some drums of fuel oil, an old fishing boat lying on its side, and a pile of rusty chain in the bushes—a scene vividly portraying the interweaving of man and nature.

As we walked to Kelly's float, piled with gasoline drums and fishnets, we could see Percy sitting quietly in the old scow with the head of his yellow dog held between his hands. The scow was gray and silver with age. Its bottom and sides were covered with fresh-cut cedar boughs.

Percy, dressed in a black foul-weather coat and hat, turned and smiled. He said Kelly would be taken up the river through the canyon. Some friends had cut a trail from the village to the cemetery the day before. We were to walk over this trail while Kelly was taken by his sons in the scow up the river to a small cove just below the cemetery.

There was a small group of people waiting on the float for the convoy of fishing boats that was bringing Kelly from town. The rain was falling in thick gray blankets and someone remarked on what a terrible day it was. Yet, in fact, it was an appropriate day, for all that could be seen—the trees, the moss, the river—was there because of the rain.

In the group on the float were fishermen, scientists from a lobster hatchery some miles away, whites and Indians. Kelly's humanity overwhelmed all contexts of race, education and all the other false barriers that hold men apart.

A close friend of Kelly's from the Fisheries Department said that only a few weeks before he and Kelly had walked up to the cemetery, and Kelly had pointed out where he wanted to be buried when his time came. It was a spot overlooking the large pool where the Henderson River makes a sharp turn before it passes through a narrow gorge or canyon and flows into the inlet. He told his friend he wanted to look down on this river scene, surrounded by mountains and trees, and watch the salmon go up river to spawn each fall.

The boats, one bearing Kelly, came down the inlet looking ghostlike as they moved in single file through the mist and rain. One . . . two . . . six . . . the rain became heavier, drowning out the noise of their engines. Then they tied up, tied up by fishermen who tie up their boats like others tie their shoes, unconsciously.

Six boats filled with friends had come to bury Kelly. No merchants of death. No hearse. No limousine. No gloves and no flowers in buttonholes. Just fishing boats and friends.

Instead of the commercial paraphernalia of death, they brought love and a compassion that caused tears to spring from a stranger's eyes. Fifty men and women came to bury their friend, with tenderness and few words. Without a pause, without advice and without help, they were putting their friend to rest. It was as if they had done it countless times during thousands of years.

Kelly was put in the scow on top of the cedar boughs and taken up the river through the gorge.

Percy followed in his dugout with his yellow dog.

The rest walked up over the hill. At first it was a narrow path through the salal, but soon, on top of the hill, there was no underbrush, just a thick blanket of moss and fallen needles. Fir, cedar, hemlock and balsam trees, giants all, dwarfed the friends of Kelly walking single file in the rain. With each step they gave evidence, on this day of death, of man's smallness and his need for friends.

As we walked over the edge of the hill two sounds, separate and distinct, could be heard. One was the rush of the river and the other was that of shovels striking the earth. A few men had preceded us and were digging Kelly's grave.

Soon it was ready, and everyone, including the dog, walked down to the river in silence. Kelly was taken from the scow and carried up the hill. The wind began to blow on the struggling rain-soaked group and the frightened yellow dog, all so small yet ageless, caught in the immensity of the trees, the mountains and the river. The words of God could hardly be heard, but of His works— the rain preparing the earth for new life and the wind tearing the yellow alder leaves from the trees—there was much evidence.

Kelly was put in the ground and covered by his friends. Then quietly the group walked back to the village, up the hill, under the giant trees and down through the salal to the fuel drums, piles of chain and the old boat lying on its side in the shallow water.

One by one the boats cast off and started down the inlet; they quickly disappeared into the rain and twilight. By early evening most of those fifty friends had returned to a modern social setting with television, supermarkets, automobiles, noise, pollution and all the opposing and antagonizing forces that permeate the daily lives of nearly all mankind.

But for a few hours, stripped of this environment, they had been people surrounded by the forces of nature, the rain and the wind and the death of a friend. That afternoon they were people of love, tenderness and compassion, no different from all the humanity that had preceded them, no matter what the millennium. Despite the myriad corroding elements in modern society—the pollution of man's dignity as well as of nature—when the occasion was provided, man showed that underneath the veneer of the twentieth century he still possesses all the ageless virtues.

These friends of Kelly brought this beauty to Kildonan, and Jack and I realized that Kildonan is not only a place but a state of mind. We do not all have to be on Uchucklesit Inlet to experience the deep forces and subtle harmonies of nature. They are in me, they are in all of us, and all this state of mind needs is an opportunity for expression. If we can find a way in our modern world for that expression, we can each find our own Kildonan.

LISA HOBBS, an award-winning journalist-by-profession, was with the *San Francisco Examiner* for ten years before joining the foreign staff of the *San Francisco Chronicle.* She studied Asian affairs at Stanford on a Professional Journalism Fellowship Award from the Ford Foundation, and in 1969 she traveled extensively in Vietnam, Laos and Cambodia. Mrs. Hobbs is well-known as a lecturer, particularly on American college campuses.

Running Towards Life is her fourth book. Her first, *I Saw Red China,* was a bestseller, a book-club selection and was translated into four languages, the Japanese edition being published by the Kajima Peace Institute.

Lisa Hobbs now lives with her family on Vancouver Island and is a feature writer for *The Vancouver Sun.*